Life Writing Series / 3

Life Writing Series

In the **Life Writing Series**, Wilfrid Laurier University Press publishes life writing and new life-writing criticism in order to promote autobiographical accounts, diaries, letters and testimonials written and/or told by women and men whose political, literary or philosophical purposes are central to their lives. **Life Writing** features the accounts of ordinary people, written in English, or translated into English from French or the languages of the First Nations or from any of the languages of immigration to Canada. **Life Writing** will also publish original theoretical investigations about life writing, as long as they are not limited to one author or text.

Priority is given to manuscripts that provide access to those voices that have not traditionally had access to the publication process.

Manuscripts of social, cultural and historical interest that are considered for the series, but are not published, are maintained in the **Life Writing Archive** of Wilfrid Laurier University Library.

Series Editor

Marlene Kadar
Humanities Division, York University

And Peace Never Came

Elisabeth M. Raab

Wilfrid Laurier University Press

This book has been published with the help of a grant in aid of publication from the Canada Council.

Canadian Cataloguing in Publication Data

Raab, Elisabeth M., 1921-
  And peace never came

(Life writing ; v. 3)
ISBN 0-88920-292-3 (pbk. with French flaps)

1. Raab, Elisabeth M., 1921- . 2. Auschwitz (Poland :
Concentration camp). 3. Holocaust, Jewish (1939-1945) –
Hungary – Personal narratives. 4. Jews – Hungary –
Biography. 5. Holocaust survivors – Canada – Biography.
I. Title. II. Series.

DS135.H93R22 1997   940.53'18'092   C96-931983-5

Copyright © 1997
WILFRID LAURIER UNIVERSITY PRESS
Waterloo, Ontario, Canada   N2L 3C5

Cover design by Leslie Macredie and Sandra Woolfrey
using photographs by Sandra Woolfrey

Cartography by Pam Schaus

Printed in Canada

Contents

Acknowledgments

My special gratitude to Sheila Robinson for her editing acumen and insight, for her consistent wise ways in prompting me to unfold enough to finish this book.

I am thankful to Maria Gould, my first teacher, for her supportive encouragement to write and to continue to do so. Many thanks to Sandra Woolfrey, director of Wilfrid Laurier University Press, for her warmth and understanding. Thanks to all my friends and family who contributed silently throughout the years by accepting my chosen solitude.

I dedicate this book to my sons, David and Robert, to their wives, Deborah and Terry, and to their children.

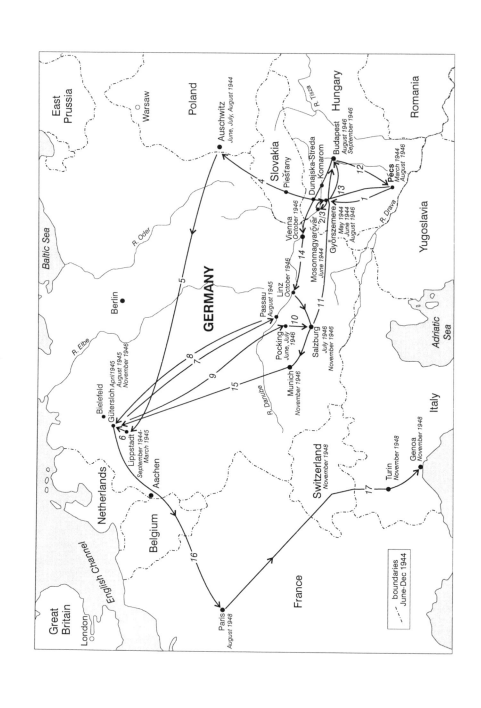

Great Britain

London

English Channel

Netherlands

Belgium

France

Switzerland
November 1948

Italy

Turin
November 1948

Genoa
November 1948

Paris
August 1948

Aachen

Lippstadt
September 1944-
March 1945

Gütersloh
August 1945
November 1946

Bielefeld
April 1945

Munich
November 1946

Pocking
June, July
1946

Salzburg
July 1946
November 1946

R. Danube

Passau
August 1945

Linz
October 1946

GERMANY

Berlin

R. Elbe

Baltic Sea

R. Oder

Poland

Warsaw

East
Prussia

Auschwitz
June, July, August 1944

Slovakia

Piešťany

Dunajska-Streda
Komarom

Mosonmagyaróvár
June 1944

Vienna
October 1946

Györszemere
May 1944
June 1944
August 1946

Budapest
August 1946
September 1946

Hungary

Pécs
March 1944
August 1946

R. Tisza

R. Drava

Yugoslavia

Romania

Adriatic
Sea

boundaries
June-Dec 1944

1
2/3
4
5
6
7
8
9
10
11
12
13
14
15
16
17

Five Years' Passage

Prologue

Why?

Why am I writing this now after so much time has gone by? Why now, when what happened has become common knowledge? Why now, when the sufferings in the world have lost their ability to shock us, when inhumanity and atrocity are no longer any secret? Why *my* story, when there are countless others who suffered as much or more?

From the moment I started to uncoil and allow myself to think about the past, I realized that forty-three years had passed since I regained my freedom; it has taken me this long to acknowledge that the past holds the present out of my reach, and that I am still not free. This is simply my story, my life.

Our Window

We often stand at the window, our favourite place, looking out with trusting tenderness toward the stamped-down, sandy roads of our village, Szemere, in the Transdanubia of Hungary. Springtime or winter, sunshine or snowfall, trees bare or rich with leaves, we are at one with the calmness of the view. My father's arm is around my shoulders; we sway to his humming, to the rhythms of operettas by Lehar, Strauss or Kalman: *Csardas Princess*, *Merry Widow*, *Gypsy Baron*, *Princess Marica*. They radiate the promise of a beautiful world ahead.

Nora

She is not with us anymore. "Nora passed away peacefully in her sleep" was the message that travelled through the ether from overseas. Was there a better way to say it? A gentler way to bring the news to me? Why didn't I stay with her longer on my last visit? She wanted me to stay.

I think about her now, resting my eyes on the view of the treetops in our backyard in Toronto. I muse about being away from Hungary since 1944, the interruptions, the changes, the disconnected, unbeaten paths between then and now: unmendable.

———

She was young, just about graduating age, when she heard the news: "Olga has a daughter."

On her way to catch the train to school, Nora stopped to see the new baby with her own eyes, on that hot morning in July. Nora: my father's younger cousin.

As she was approaching the house, friends of my parents arrived, sidetracked on their way home from an all-night party at "Zöld Major" farm, a few miles out of town. Equipped with a gypsy band, they stopped for a serenade under my parents' bedroom window.

A serenade is a nocturnal event and is usually a means of expressing admiration. The recipient is supposed to light a candle behind the curtain for a moment in acknowledgment. My father had no candle, nor any need of one; it was already 7:00 in the morning. He laughingly picked up the tiny bundle and held it aloft close to the window, in acknowledgment of the serenade.

I heard the story of my own birth many times. The last person alive to remember it was Nora.

I recall the last time I saw her a few years ago. As always, as soon as she opened the door, her first words were, "Now you will stay with me for a while. I won't let you go." She said that while standing in the doorway, supporting her back on the door frame.

For years an unknown ailment had cast its shadow on her. Nevertheless, she went on with her life with gracious, stoic calm, disregarding her discomfort, holding on to her inherited rules and principles. She succeeded so well that in the course of the years we often asked ourselves if her problems were imaginary or real. After extensive investigation, her son-in-law discovered that they were very real indeed. The name of her illness was never spelled out, though in our narrow circle we knew. Nora calmly accepted her lot as if it were a natural process in life. Daisy and Walter, her daughter and son-in-law, living abroad, spared no effort to keep a steady long-distance eye on her through friends and doctors in Nora's faraway little town. Their care kept her reasonably comfortable and extended her tranquil life for over ten years.

It is a sad-looking town where Nora found refuge after the war, as if beauty had no place in the creation of a Communist society. Apart from a few older houses, there are mostly four-to-five-storey row houses for workers, thrown together from concrete blocks. They are bunched around untidy, open parking lots; all were built with the goal of merely putting roofs over people's heads. The picture repeats itself through the town monotonously.

Nora lived here in one of them.

Approaching the neglected lots, I was overcome with gloom and dread. I entered the rusty door to the stairway. My steps echoed harshly as I climbed the bare stone stairs. Repairing the unwashed, broken windows was nobody's business.

Not until Nora opened her door with a warm welcoming smile was I able to leave the soulless exterior behind.

The apartment was only large enough for one person's minimal needs but, once inside, you felt her presence in every last corner. It was whole and complete; the doilies, curtains, pictures, plants and furniture in that single room were in harmony with her personality, with her stately self-respect. They were like a living part of her.

Whenever I asked, "How are you, Aunt Nora? How are things around here?" her answer was always a steady, "I am fine. I have what I need. Anybody who says differently isn't telling the truth. That doesn't mean we're rich, but everyone can live, and nobody has to go hungry. That we have to grant to Communism."

I always had difficulty choosing a gift to take to her. The easiest would have been money, but I didn't dare, she was so proud. Most of the time my eventual choice was a dainty blouse. She used to put it on, honouring it while I was there. "Look how beautifully it goes with my suit," she would remark. "And the blouse from the last time," she opened her armoire, "isn't it perfect with my blue suit?"

Her favourite attire: the suit. It looked good on her, on her slender figure, as if they'd been made for each other. Sleekness and modesty were the qualities that emanated from Nora, not from her clothing and hairdo alone, but from her entire attitude and behaviour, even from her smooth, well-considered movements.

She had been brought up by her mother, Flora, who led her five children into adulthood. Her father had died when she was still a child. Nora was the youngest of the five and the closest to her mother.

Those were times when a young girl had to have the self-discipline to sit, if necessary, "throughout a whole day's trip, and keep her immaculate white gloves on." She told me that many years ago, with relish.

In her later years she liked to tell me other stories, too, but for some reason she repeated this one on my visits. "I was walking with Zsiga"—then her fiancé—"in the yard, when suddenly you popped out from a stable door. 'What are you doing, little girl?' I asked, and you said, 'I just watched the little colt jumping out of his mummy'. . . ."

I remembered, too, when my mother had to go to town and took my doll with her "to bring me a new one." To my joy, she left me with Nora. She was kind and quiet-voiced; it was easy to be with her. I followed her around happily; only my doll caused me disappointment when it came. My mother and Nora glanced at each other, I noticed, seeing my aversion to the doll's garish yellow hair. I found out later that it was the same old doll with new, artificial-smelling, silky hair.

In those days, everything had to be used to the last thread, even the socks. They were mended and mended again over the mending. My mother wasted no time in introducing me to the art of mending; I was only five. As I was sitting on my lawn chair in front of our house, absorbed in trying the darning trade, I heard, "Oh please, Böske, you should never learn that." Astonished, I looked up. A rebellious outburst like that I didn't expect from Nora, but if she said it, I thought, she must have been right. Her three brothers produced enough socks to mend, and that was her job.

I did not remind her of this episode, though I would have loved to, and would have loved to reminisce with her about old times, mainly about people I felt close to then, but wasn't mature enough really to know.

My visits to her, four in all, were stolen times from European trips, or from family life. I couldn't find a way to explain my deep attachment to her and to make it understandable at home. The absence of my family's approval was a hidden apprehension in my short stays, while she was pressing me to stay longer. I was aware that my visits brought change and freshness to her everyday life, and provided, for both of us, a short trip to the past: for her, to her youth, and for me, to my childhood.

I had not much time to ask questions. She loved to remember stories and I listened gladly to what she had to tell me. She reminded me of this: "You know the picture where you were hiding in an armchair, you were about three? I took that with me when I got married. That picture was our ideal of a child. Zsiga and I kept pinching it from each other's night tables."

After hearing this story, it came back to me how I had accepted Zsiga instantly as "Nora's friend." To be the first to see him, I hid under the seat in the landau when the coachman went to pick up Zsiga at the station. That was on one of his visits before they were married.

Zsiga was a well-to-do gentleman, as I recall, with dark hair, reassuring brown eyes, the usual farmer's florid complexion from the fresh air; he wore a moustache. He was of average height and always well groomed. One got the impression of a jovial uncle rather than a dashing cavalier. Nora was twenty years his junior.

Then came the trip to Vienna for Nora, the bride-to-be. In Zsiga's opinion, it had to be Vienna, "the only worthy place to shop." He didn't let Nora or her mother, Flora, skimp: "It had to be the best."

I listened, speechless, to the wondrous tale, told as only Aunt Flora could tell it. In excited awe, silently, I looked at—but didn't touch—the graceful luxuries, the elegant wool and silk dresses, some for the morning, some for the early

9

afternoon, others for after five, still more for dinner and some for late evenings; a wraparound fur coat, and a black coat with a huge silver-fox collar, scarves, gloves, more and more, all so soft, and smelling so good . . . I thought, How wonderful it must be to be grown up. I asked Nora carefully, "Aunt Nora, will you give these to me when I'm grown up?" She drew me close and said with her calm smile, "Yes, Böske, I will."

After their honeymoon in Capri they went back to Zsiga's estate in Czechoslovakia to live. There was a border to cross to Hungary, but she still lived close to her mother and, therefore, close to us, too.

Nora came back to stay with her mother before her daughter, Daisy, was born. I was overjoyed to see her, and the only things I wanted were to listen to every word she uttered about her new world, be close to her, and touch the glamorous shiny dressing gown she wore.

And now my thoughts turn to 1930, to the days of our hope and prayers for Zsiga, and to the disheartening acceptance—the first in my life—of something final and hopelessly unchangeable. Zsiga died in Vienna of blood poisoning from an infected tooth.

Nora was back at her mother's with her baby. She was all in black and very sad. I remember my own sadness and the pain I felt at seeing her grief. After some time, she returned to her life in Czechoslovakia, trying to take the place of Zsiga, who had been the driving force there.

After being alone for years, she married a very nice man, Sandor, but I doubt he could ever have made up for her loss. Later a son, Peter, was born.

Then war came dangerously close, and when it caught up with us we didn't see each other until twenty-seven years later (in 1971), when at last I could afford to travel back to Hungary from Canada.

It was comforting to find that Nora had remained essentially the same. The only difference came from the dramatic changes in our lives, but she spoke and acted just as she always had.

My coming was a surprise to her, and after that first visit I arranged every visit as a surprise, so as not to excite her unnecessarily ahead of time.

After we had sat down and discussed how long I would stay, she would rush to the phone to let her son, Peter, know the news. I would hear her leaving the message in his office to come home, for he was usually out of town. Nevertheless, he appeared every time after an hour or two. When I asked, "Why are you home? How did you know I was here?" his answer was, "Everybody knows, the whole county knows. They phoned for me everywhere. If my mother calls, everybody stands at attention."

In the evening of my first visit, seeing the bed she had made for me, I was close to weeping. The ironed linen pillows and sheets, starched to a silky shine and put there just so, spoke to me at once about delicate treatment and care, about respect and devotion, about beauty and tradition. It was as if a lost treasure had come alive in front of me.

We went to bed and talked till late, or rather Nora did, because I could hardly talk; I was so overwhelmed.

I was woken early by: "Oh, I am so glad you slept well." Dear, good Nora was eager to go on with our reunion.

"Yes, I had a very good night. I slept, somehow feeling protected. Actually I felt as I felt only back in Szemere."

"Maybe you had a good reason to feel like that; the eiderdown pillow you slept on is from Szemere."

Then Edith, the woman who worked for Nora, knocked. Before opening the door, Nora put her dressing gown on with slow, measured movements, long familiar to me. I heard her saying with a special gleam in her voice, "Edith, you won't guess who I have here."

They sat down in the kitchen—I could hear it from the bedroom—to talk over the plans for the day. "Edith, we need

11

that and that . . . pick up at the grocer's . . . and tell the tailor . . . and what fruit do we need . . . make sure you put Böske's pillow on the top, she may want to lie down in the afternoon. . . ."

The sound of that audience took me back again in years. "How did you get Edith?" I asked. "Years ago her mother was a very good maid of mine," she said.

A curious set-up in a Communist country, but everybody seemed to respect this grand lady. Peter told me how, to his embarrassment, Nora scolded the county's Party Secretary, but the Chief just smiled at her.

When I came back to Canada in 1987 I brought a pillow with me, a surprise present she had sewn by hand while I was out with Peter. It was made out of the eiderdown from Szemere.

The last time I visited Nora, in 1989, she received me at the door with a smile, as always. She was leaning against the doorframe, with her back bent, for support. She hugged me and looked at me by lifting her eyelids, forcing her eyes upward. She couldn't lift her head; her neck was parallel with the floor. A shocking change from when I had seen her last.

I hugged her and smiled too and asked, needlessly, how she was. She didn't give me any explanation or complaints. Then came: "Now you stay with me for awhile, I won't let you go." She said that resolutely. I smiled without answering.

I felt uneasy. I knew I had to lie. As the hours sped by, I felt my will to stay crumbling, failing me. I could not stand the pain of being with her . . . I could hardly bear the pain and guilt of leaving . . . but I left. I stayed only a few hours. I could have stayed the night. I could have stayed much longer. But no, I had to leave.

Poor, dear Nora, how could she guess my torment, how could she see my inner conflict? She never had to change, she remained always close to her origins. A visit with her meant a visit to my inner world, a visit to my past life, my other self.

And I could not bring the inside and the outside close enough to meet. Ever.

I called a day later from Budapest. I wanted to hear that she didn't hold a grudge, that she was all right.

"How are you, Aunt Nora?"

"If you can only come for a few hours, then it's better you don't come," was her answer.

———

I am sitting at home in Toronto, on the second floor of my house. I look out into the backyard, at the garden, the neighbouring fences, the friendly roofs, the back windows, the slightly moving trees.

The sun is still shining though it has already reached the west. It is a late afternoon in October. My grandson Daniel's little white bed is next to me. On the quilt are red, yellow, blue, and green balloons.

A loving glance back through my memory to the fragrant kid gloves, to the silver-fox collar, luxurious and warm to bury my face in. "Will you give these to me when I'm grown up?"

Who in Their Right Mind . . . ?

E ver since the beginning of the 1930s we have heard the thunder from within the German borders; it has echoed as far east as Hungary and beyond, but we don't believe it will develop into a full-fledged storm. Naively, we tell ourselves that the blustering, the fist-brandishing demagoguery against the Jews, is clearly recognizable as a self-serving show. We think the noisy and absurd lies will burst like soap bubbles as soon as the rest of the world takes notice. Who in their right mind, we ask each other, can believe in a campaign of slander better suited to the early Middle Ages than to twentieth-century Europe?

———

March 1938. The Germans boldly annex Austria, marching in, in full view of the whole world. "Anschluss," they call it. The Austrian border is only eighty-odd kilometres west of Szemere, my hometown in Hungary. Still, we insist it doesn't concern us. The upheaval will settle. Hitler, as he says, only wants German-speaking Austria. We believe our own tale and go about our daily lives as before. The only change is that we begin to listen more alertly and with some concern to the news coming from the West.

On April 11, my mother, with great prudence, fills my suitcase neatly with practical clothes—skirts and blouses—that she thinks a sixteen-year-old girl travelling with her classmates to Italy for a two-week art trip might need.

I board the express train at six o'clock in the evening when it stops briefly in my small town and I run towards its lowered windows where the girls are hanging out, waving, cheering, expecting me to join them. I run in my navy blue suit (my mother always dresses me in navy) and pale pink blouse. Hard behind me, and probably just as excited, is good old Pista, our coachman, who helps carry my black patent suitcase onto the train.

The girls pull me into the compartment, into the ongoing hubbub, where after a short assessment of the prevailing situation I begin to fit in with their high spirits. We chat away excitedly as the train rushes southwards through Austria, Graz, Klagenfurt, until fatigue numbs the edge of our expectations. Unwillingly we doze, leaning against the head rests. I lean against the wall of my window seat, behind the closed curtain, jostled from my sleep every time the train slows or stops. From time to time I wake and peek out, sleep-dazed, into the dark, but only long enough to decipher what I take to be the station's name: "Uscita." Then my head falls back against the wall, into oblivion. At every jerky stop or start, I open my eyes and read the same name, "Uscita." After some time I wonder aloud at this senseless stagnation in the same city, not realizing yet that what I keep reading is "Exit" in Italian.

The train cuts southward through the high Alps, between the awesomely severe peaks of the Dolomites, leaving hundreds of echoes behind. In the morning, we catch our first glimpse of the azure Adriatic Sea melting into the blue sky at Trieste. At two in the afternoon, in a balmy, drunken mood from lack of sleep, we disembark at Venice's stunning, modern railway station. It is white, sleek and monumental, like a holy temple, breathtakingly alien after my narrow world, which until now has consisted only of Hungary. Later, seeing more such stations, I realize that they were built to give the appearance of prosperity, as window dressing for Italian fascism.

We spend one rest day in Venice, then travel on for a longer stay in Florence and its famous environs. Face to face with great art for the first time, we listen carefully to the teacher/guide to grasp some of its marvels. We learn the melodious names, exotic to our young Hungarian ears: Uffizi, Palazzo Pitti, Boboli Gardens, Tiziano, Raffaello and Michelangelo. On a free afternoon, we haggle over souvenirs with vendors on the Ponte Vecchio. We approach these vendors in groups, as the exciting news spreads that they think we are bargaining for their goods. We find bargaining is the norm here, and our lack of Italian is no problem. Bursting with laughter, we recite Hungarian poems, and after every line, the price is lowered.

Our next stop is Bologna, then a short stay in Padua before returning to Venice. Among other artistic and historic spots, we visit St. Antonio's Basilica and the saint's tomb in Padua. While there, we buy the usual souvenir, the saint's miniature statue in a small silver case. It is a good luck charm. To make it work we hold it against the wall of the tomb for a while. All of us, including the Jewish students, take the sanctifying very seriously. When I have finished with mine, I notice a friend who solemnly holds hers to the wall, totally involved. Our Jewish Studies teacher, who has accompanied us on the trip, walks up behind her with a faint smile. I hear him whisper, "Miss Weiner, isn't it holy enough yet?"

We visit the artistic and historic sites, but we also walk on Italy's streets and see the rushing burghers going about their daily lives. Among other things, I notice and ridicule the pompous, uniformed Blackshirts. We think of their parading as part of bombastic Mussolini's not-to-be-taken-too-seriously politics. I also observe and admire the lilac bushes, blooming a month earlier here than at home. This spring, they'll bloom twice for me.

17

A boring train trip becomes livelier as we approach Bologna and discover two young men in the corridor in front of our compartment. Some of the girls immediately start up a conversation. Our teachers endeavour to keep us away from the other passengers, which only makes our illicit conversation more exciting. As the train comes into the station, the young men help all the girls except me with their luggage. At first I wonder why I have been left out, until finally one of them takes mine, too. Then they lean out the window to wave goodbye to us as we descend the stairs into the Bologna underpass. One of the young men is clearly waving to me. I don't dare wave back. Still, the girls all notice. Giggling, they babble the news around the group and elbow me suggestively.

Our last stop after Bologna is a return trip to Venice. We wonder at the beauty of the city: the Rialto Bridge, the gondolas, the Lido. We listen with awe to our teachers inside St. Mark's Cathedral, and marvel at the opulence of it. Glancing to one side, I discover we are standing near the two young men from the train.

Later, at Scuole, they appear again. We visit the Doge's Palace, inside and out, and as I walk over to admire the fountain in the middle of the courtyard, there they are again.

On our last night in Venice, we say goodbye with a special evening outing—ice cream at the Quadrillo, on the Piazza San Marco. We finish off the evening with a walk under the full moon, passing the Campanile to the Grand Canal, watching the *vaporettos* arrive. As we walk slowly, two by two, one of our young men suddenly appears and cuts his way through to me and puts a note in my hand. I keep it as secret as possible and only unfold it later in my hotel room. His name is on it and his address: Häbel Strausse 17, Basel, Switzerland. Puzzled, I read the few words he has written. "Can you . . . ?" Then I stick it in with the rest of my souvenirs from Italy.

———

April 23, 1938. On my return to Hungary, I find things have changed. An anti-Jewish bill has become law, and is enacted later in May. From then on, no Jewish men or women can be hired for work. Practically, it means that recently graduated students are unable to find jobs. In addition, the existing contingent of employed Jews must be reduced every six months. All Jewish public employees, including teachers, are dismissed. We take the fact that independent businesses or self-employed workers are left alone as an indication that the Hungarian government has no intention of harming us. We are convinced that their law is a pro forma measure on the government's part to keep the Germans away with small decoys. That is how we interpret the new politics. "It will pass," is our watchword. "It is a matter of waiting it out." And so we do nothing. Rather than facing the current realities, my teenage mind dwells on my memories of Italy. I trust my home and feel safe about my future. One day I remember the note from Venice and think, Why not make Italy last a bit longer? I write a letter to Switzerland and my father lets me mail it, after a long explanation on my part. Just a few days later, I find a reply (already opened by parental censorship) on my desk. The reply. I read and reread it, amazed that he answered and at the snapshots that fall out of it. Snapshots of me. I realize he took them, unnoticed, in Venice.

Interestingly, the young man is from Hungary. He writes that he is a Calvinist theology student studying in Basel. I write back, and an intense correspondence begins; we exchange letters twice a week. There is no objection on my parents' part. Apparently they enjoy reading the letters, too. Towards the end of the school year, he lets me know his plans for the summer. He would like to visit us at our home. I become very concerned, knowing I have to respond and provide a serious answer. I realize that, besides being Hungarian, I am also Jewish, and I have to tell him. I am sure he understands the temporary misconception of the Jews as much as I do, but I also see there is no future in our friendship. After all, he is a Calvinist theology student. I write to him that I am Jewish. The answer comes back promptly, as usual. My mother hands it to me over the table, open as always, and she remains sitting there with a sock to darn in her hands. I read it. I finish and look up at her through my tears. She is trying to hide her own from me. That is the first time I have seen her like that.

In his letter he asks me to write. But I never send a reply. I feel words won't make it better.

————

One afternoon in late spring my mother tells me we are expecting visitors for afternoon coffee. Our coachman picks them up at the railway station. We spend a pleasant afternoon, during which I am introduced to a young man. Actually he doesn't seem that young to me, since I am used to men only two or three years older than me. Imre Hoffmann is fourteen years my senior. He keeps up a steady conversation with me, and I listen the way it is expected I should, while we all go out for a walk in the garden after coffee. He tells me about his well-established, prosperous wholesale chocolate business in Pécs, a city about four hundred kilometres by train from Szemere. I hear him telling my parents about it, too. And then my father is invited to Pécs, where he travels one or two weeks later.

In spite of personal reservations that I can only guess at, my parents give in to his marriage proposal. Imre is thirty years old. I am seventeen. Suddenly everything changes around me. I am lifted from my teenage world to the higher, important world of adulthood. I am treated as an adult by family and friends of the family, and I am supposed to fit into my role instantly, without preparation. I am pampered by the steady arrival of chocolates and flowers by special delivery. I am kept busy with letters I have received that are handed over to me unopened and unread by my parents. I am flattered, overpowered by all the attention which came to me so unexpectedly. Suddenly, I am consulted in planning what clothes I need, and included in all the grown-ups' concerns: choosing furniture, buying beautiful linen, and in the midst of all the shopping, planning a new household. I am swept away by a seemingly easy, agreeable new lifestyle.

"Do you have to love your husband?" I ask my mother.

"With time you get used to him," is her answer. I ponder her words, considering all the commotion about me, and having no one to seek advice from. I come to terms with my marriage as a door out of Szemere into a wider world. At the same time I am secure in the knowledge that the same door will stay open for me to come back to my cradle for repose. But most importantly, I long to get away from the disturbing and ever-hovering intrigues and meddling of my relatives. In July, on my seventeenth birthday, I become engaged to Imre Hoffmann and we are married in December 1938.

———

March 1939. Shortly after our marriage, my husband is called up to the army. I take over the management of his business. It is in every way an abrupt start for me in Pécs. I am new as a wife, in a new environment, with new people, with totally new conditions to conform to. And I am thrust into a business that I have not yet had time to learn. But I go into it with my best will and tackle it wholeheartedly, in spite of the pressure, or maybe because of it, and in spite of the old employees, who jealously guard their territories.

Two months later Imre is released, but shortly afterwards he is called up again. The major part of our first married year, 1939, we live between the worrisome army service and the release from it, never knowing when the next call-up will hit. But soon I find business life most interesting and I submerge myself in it with enthusiasm. From then on, I remain a steady working partner in business.

The following year, my husband is stripped of his army uniform and his rank as a voluntarily enlisted corporal, a special status in Hungary for high-school graduates, and put into a forced labour unit. The work is hard labour, physically strenuous jobs with picks and shovels. These groups of men are easy to spot, working on railroads, on highways and in quarries, with their white armbands and in their own civilian clothes, their faces conspicuously unfitted for such work.

Some inmates of the labour unit stayed in Hungary, but most are sent into the Russian winter under the supervision of a Hungarian crew, simple-minded footsoldiers who believe what they are told: "the sooner you finish off the Jews the earlier you get home." Imre stays in the country. If his unit is nearby he is able to spend some weekends at home. Otherwise we are apart.

Often on my own, I feel lucky to meet people who become precious to me, both my age and also older. With some I become close friends. It disturbs me, though, that my husband can't seem to accept my desire to have people around me. He wants me isolated, away from everyone. In spite of that, I don't give up my friends. I also visit my parents as often as I can because I feel my real home is still with them in Szemere. Only years later do I mention my difficulties with Imre to my parents. "Let's see what the end of the war brings," they reply.

June 1941. The German-Russian war starts. We react to the news almost with enthusiasm, seeing in it Germany's approaching defeat, perhaps even soon. Some draw a parallel between Napoleon's disastrous campaign in Russia and this one. Hungarian politics also shows a slight shift away from the "Axis," with some placatory leaning toward the West. My husband is released unexpectedly from forced labour and spends close to a year at home. We both believe the times are changing for the better.

On April 26, 1942, my husband is called up again. My first baby is due any day, but he has to leave immediately. The next day, April 27, my daughter, Katalin Judith, is born. The following day, still in bed in the maternity ward, I spot my mother, unexpectedly, through the open door, pacing impatiently, waiting to be allowed in. In an instant, when she wipes her tears away, our eyes meet. I know that now I am allowed to collapse. My natural link, my reliance on my parents, gives me this relief. It is as if I were at home again. She gives her support in my household for four weeks. In my first insecure steps with the baby, she helps me with her advice. She tries to shield me in every way. At the same time, approvingly, she compares modern times with her own when she was pampered in bed for four weeks after childbirth. I go back to work after one week.

In my mind, business has to go on. I carry total responsibility for it and take it very seriously. I become an utterly different person from the inexperienced novice I was when I first tried to tackle its mysteries. I grow up, and grow into a business enthusiast. I work wholeheartedly during business hours, from 8 a.m. to 8 p.m., six days a week, but manage to be free from its worries as soon as I arrive home or am with friends. During these years I gradually become someone to visit at work. Visitors drop in to see me during all business hours, and the number of visitors grows as time goes on and as my circle of acquaintances in Pécs widens. I have not much time for conversation while I deal with customers, order merchandise, telephone, or dispatch orders, but a few words of acknowledgment or a smile seems sufficient to my guests, whoever they happen to be. Maybe it's my looks, my youth, my exceptional business acumen, or maybe all these things together that make me a novelty. I am innocently unaware of the reason for people's interest until someone says, "I have to bring my daughter in to meet you," or I hear remarks such as, "What a businesswoman." But I know I am not a businesswoman in the conventional sense they think I am. I only look like one. I am enthusiastic about being with people. I am here because I see in business something other than money, and I see the performance I put on as an art. My goal is to please. In dealing with my customers, I keep in mind their interests above all. My idealistic view of business, which has turned into success, spurs me on. I go on happily, with joie de vivre. I am able to share my belief that life can be pleasant even if it is serious, and that it is possible to put business dealings into a higher sphere if only we are kinder and more open with each other.

When my mother leaves, Ditta, my cousin, stays with Kati and me and my help in the house, Margit. Ditta stays until the end of 1943; then she moves to Budapest, thinking she will have more opportunity there.

———

March 19, 1944. It is a balmy Sunday spring morning. Expecting that someone might drop by in the afternoon, I take out the ingredients for a cheese strudel. As I start to pull the dough out, to make it artistically thin, someone knocks at the door. My hands dredged with flour, I open it. A friend stands there, hardly able to speak:

"The Germans occupied Hungary during the night." Her words reverberate around me like a bolt of thunder. I feel as if it were the last seconds before an inevitable disaster. What's next?

Coming to life, I pack my whole household into wooden boxes and wicker trunks and pile it all up in one room. I lock up the business and leave the key with friends. Without saying goodbye to anyone, Kati and I leave by train for my parents' on March 21. My only thought is that we must be together. All of us. Who knows what the future holds? I can't think of anything else to do. Szemere was always a haven. I keep relying on the past.

Margit is our only companion on the trip, dressed up in my clothes and in my hat. I sit next to her, dressed simply and modestly. At one of the stations, German soldiers get on. They are loud and arrogant, as if it were their right to occupy most of the seats, as if they were in their full rights to be there. Margit looks at me questioningly when they take the seats next to me. Her face flushes red. I reply with a calming glance, although I don't know myself what lies ahead. Soon they start up a conversation about Saloniki, Greece, where they are coming from right now. I am boiling inwardly. I think with sympathy of German-occupied Saloniki. Outwardly, I am collected and calm, giving relaxed answers to their questions. For instance, where do I live? Where did I learn German? They even suggest they would like to visit me. Throughout the four-hundred-kilometre trip I am very much aware of the risk I take by travelling. Jews are prohibited to travel except with a special permit. They must also wear a yellow star. I have neither. But, by instinct more than planning, I take secondary train routes and we arrive safely at my parents'. The next day I send Margit back with orders to remain in my home in Pécs.

Our arrival in Szemere is not joyous as it usually is. I no sooner arrive than disturbing, confusing questions are thrown at me: "Where is your brother Miki?" "Where is your cousin Ditta?"

"I don't know," I reply. "What makes you think we should have come together?"

"Because on March 19 we sent a telegraph to them saying 'Return home immediately.'" The family doesn't know what to think. In fact, we don't dare to think anything at all. We only hope silently that everything will turn out well. A few weeks later a friend writes that he has traced their whereabouts. Miki and Ditta are in a camp in Hungary. Apparently they were arrested by the Gestapo at the station, boarding the train on their way to Szemere. Furthermore, the friend writes, through a Jewish organization it is possible to send a food parcel to them in the camp. We are overjoyed by that meagre piece of news. My mother starts to bake scones without delay. She puts her whole heart and all the anxieties of the past few weeks, along with her prayers, into the parcel and we mail it right away. Unknown to us, they are already in Auschwitz. They never receive it.

With the German occupation of Hungary, the American and British bombardment begins. They come in massive waves, flying overhead day and night. During the day, I look up to the sky ever-so-thankfully, to the glittering silvery planes in the spring sunshine. I know they are the Americans. I am choked with tears for the two American pilots parachuting from their burning plane over Szemere. I follow their silent descent to earth from the peaceful April sky, until they hit down somewhere behind a hill. I can hardly stand the pain when I hear that they were clubbed to death with the stock of a rifle by the Hungarian gendarmes.

At night, my Kati sleeps her honest, trustful baby sleep in her crib close to me. I listen in the dark to the solid roaring from the sky, breathing hope with my sighs. I wish them well. They are the British. They are so close, yet so far.

In an unguarded moment I say to my parents: "I would prefer to die from an English or American bomb than fall into German hands."

"How can you say such a thing in front of your mother," reproaches my father when we are alone.

Hungarian industry cautiously hides its important employees and offices in smaller towns. Ours is no exception, which is how a wonderful family is assigned to our house, Gyula and Anna and their two little daughters. Their warm, calm, supportive presence, without useless words, is precious to me and to my parents. They lend me enough of their values to keep my self unbroken and proud through the next two tormenting months in Szemere. And many more beyond that. I have been thankful ever since.

After a week in Szemere I realize I have handled matters unwisely by rushing from Pécs under the first shock. I leave my daughter Kati with my parents and risk a trip back. There, I give the business over to a very dear friend who has been out of a job since the new rules regarding hiring Jews came into effect. At home, I pack some suitcases with my most important belongings to take to Szemere with me. Margit remains in Pécs. Again I travel without the necessary papers and without the yellow star. In my mind the yellow star serves as an open invitation to the Nazis. Upon my safe appearance back in Szemere, my parents, Anna and Gyula literally jump and applaud in relief. I have been away three days and they worried the whole time.

From then on, every day brings new restrictions, new laws successively tightening a rope around us, pushing us away from normal life. With helpless inertia we let it happen. Incredulous, we watch the menacing fingers pointing at us, "the Jews, the hated evils, rightly condemned by the just world." All day the inflammatory propaganda is fed to the ignorant, to those who are ready to hate.

At night German soldiers break in on us. They are not even the brutes of the Gestapo unit. They are from the Wehrmacht, the regular front soldiers. Local people show them the way. The Gestapo strikes in the daytime, cruising incessantly around like a school of sharks. We never know who they will take next. They come to our house, too, a few times, looking for something—anything—for some reason to torture and arrest. One time they claim they are searching for a receiver of foreign broadcasts. Finding nothing in the house, they take the poor coachman's small homemade radio from the stalls.

I suggest to my father the idea of going into hiding, but the thought seems totally alien to him, even unreasonable. He thinks we will be able to wait it out. I drop the matter, concluding that he may be right.

On May 12, the order comes to leave. We are to join other Jews about seventy kilometres away in the small city of Magyaróvár, close to the Austrian border. We can hardly believe it. Meanwhile, a delegation of farmers, led by the head of the Nazi Party in Szemere, travels to the District Attorney with a request for an exemption for my daughter and me. The supposed reason is that I am needed as a cook for the farm hands; the request is refused. We are given four days to prepare for the trip. When we are done, we have three horsedrawn carriages loaded with the belongings we think we'll need, wherever we might go. At the last minute I rummage and sort through my personal things, coming across my new hat. It is a Durbin, the newest fashion, named after the hat Deanna Durbin wore in her latest film. I bought it for the spring to wear with my new tweed suit, but I've never worn it. With a sudden desire to try it, I put it on and look into the mirror. As I lift my eyes to the hat, I notice Gyula standing behind me further back in the doorway. Ashamed of my vanity, I pull the hat off gruffly and throw it aside. He says, "It looks beautiful on you." His eyes betray an infinite sadness. I move on. I pretend not to understand why.

While we get ready for the trip, Anna and Gyula go through difficult days, too. Like us, they can't find peace in the house. We sort and pack and make hard decisions about what to take, from what to part. We must leave much behind. Years of history, precious memorabilia, photographs, dear memories. Anna, noticing the prayer books on the shelves, says to me: "Why don't you destroy them? Burn them. Who will take care of them? In whose hands will they end up?" I don't mention her harsh suggestion to my parents. And, out of piety, I don't have the heart to destroy them.

The lilacs are in full bloom. I run out into the garden to fill my mother's cobalt vase, and put the blooms in a room among piled-up furniture. On the morning of May 16, on my mother's forty-ninth birthday, my mother, my father, my two-year-old daughter and I are taken for the last time out of our yard. Out of Szemere. On top of a horsedrawn wagon, we are evicted, taken through the streets, out of the town. No one is out; or maybe they are simply behind the curtains. An epoch is closing. This is its end.

"I'll never be here again," my mother says.

The Narrowing Circle

On the way to Magyaróvár, the gendarmes stop the horse-drawn wagons and read aloud the names on their list. Neither my name nor Kati's is read out. The District Attorney left our names off, but didn't dare to tell us. And now I am there with the others. My smart Aunt Flora says, "Böske, don't be a fool. Disappear from here." My parents say nothing. I don't know what to do. Finally the gendarme asks me who I am and then writes our names with the rest on the list.

We arrive in Magyaróvár late that afternoon and are billeted in the home of a Jewish family. Our wagons are unloaded and the men and horses return to Szemere. The owner of the house makes room for us for the night after this day of anguish and uncertainty.

Our stay in that home is short, only ten days. Just as we are beginning to accommodate ourselves to a new way of life, we are condemned to move again, and this time we have to abandon most of our possessions. We are moved to a narrow, more concentrated compound. Close to a thousand people are crowded together, compelled to share rooms, pressed closely with strangers. Hygienic conditions are non-existent, and there is hardly any food.

Peace is not to be granted to us here, either. Suddenly one morning, after hardly a week, we are ordered to pack. It happens from one moment to the next. And this time one suitcase or parcel is the maximum we can take. We arrive at the railway station on foot and climb into the waiting boxcars. But before we climb up, my father remembers that he left his fur-lined winter coat behind. Still thinking that we are in a civilized country, he asks the gendarme to allow him to go and pick it up. His request is promptly rejected. I feign not seeing this embarrassing fiasco.

Hours later, in the dry heat of the late afternoon, the train stops. When we are ordered to move, we find ourselves on a hidden length of railway track in Győr. Surrounded by armed gendarmes, and carrying what last remnants of our possessions we still have, we continue on foot. Where are we going? Who knows? On my arm I carry Kati, and on my back, in a bundle, our last needs. As I walk heavily, my eyes on the ground, I feel somebody by my side keeping pace with me. I don't even look. I don't care.

"Give me the little girl, I'll help you carry her," says a voice. I turn to see a young man from Szemere, probably on his way home from work, holding the handle bars of his bicycle. Touched by his humanity, I nearly break down. I give my Kati to him, but he takes only a few steps before a gendarme walks up and forbids him to hold her. The soldier takes the child from the young man's arms and gives her back to me. The man walks quickly away from me, pushing his bicycle, his face flushed. Ashamed. He hasn't altered his values yet; he is still ignorant of the times. I hope this one mistake won't damage him.

We arrive at a fenced-in place, which we have never seen before, just at dusk. We are commanded to go one by one through a gate, past a gendarme who counts us in like cattle being driven into barn. Matches or candles are taken away, if we have them. In the meantime it is getting darker, but we can still distinguish the low buildings into which we are being sent.

In pitch-black rooms we find ourselves advancing in the dark, step by step, with arms stretched out tentatively before us. Exhausted, we sit down on the floor, only to find ourselves on wet, rotting straw. In the morning we realize we are fenced into a desolate, rundown ghetto area on the outskirts of Győr. This is to be our home for the next ten days.

We spend only one Friday in the ghetto. Led by Dr. Roth, a respected young rabbi in Győr, the elders organize a Friday evening service. We gather, all five thousand inhabitants of the ghetto, under the open sky, for a moment of release from despair. We are joined in a sense of community. We are momentarily not alone; we are joined in our spirits.

The next morning, Saturday, we awaken to find all the rabbis lined up outside. Bloodied, beaten, their faces green and blue. They are ridiculed. The shape of a star is cut into their scalps. The shape shows starkly against their terrifying white scalps. The Jewish star. Between the Gestapo men, armed with clubs, they are paraded and chased through the whole ghetto. We stand in terror, in bewilderment. The only sound is the laughter of the SS. We stand in deadly silence.

After a few minutes, I notice my father. In spite of what has just happened, he insists on maintaining a pretence of normalcy. Not only can he not face the reality of our situation, he does not want to admit it to me. He maintains the pretext of seeing beauty and benignity where there is none. He faces me cautiously, embarrassed by the world's cruelty and ugliness. But the truth is impossible to escape anymore. Shame, worry, sadness pass over his eyes when he sees the horror on my face. I feel I have given up on nobility and am unable to pretend. Strangely, my strongest emotions are a sense of embarrassment and guilt in front of him.

———

June 17, 1944. We are moved from the ghetto to the railway again. Sometime during our second night on the train, Hungarian gendarmes break the lock and storm in on us in the cattle car. There we sit cramped on the floor in inky darkness. They are yelling: "This is the last demand for all your valuables: money, gold, silver, leather. Whoever violates this order will be severely punished."

I know my mother has hidden a small silver comb. Otherwise we have nothing, not even water or food. The comb was a gift from my brother Miki, whose whereabouts have been unknown to us since the Germans captured him months ago. I make a prompting sign to her. She whispers to me firmly, "Whatever happens, I won't give that up."

———

My father is the only one who is tall enough to look out the high wired opening in the cattle car. "Here in Krakow was where we were sent to the Russian front in the First World War," he reports. I think about the terrible Russian front where he was wounded in 1916. He spoke sometimes with old comrades about it. For that he received the "Iron Cross," a respected military decoration. They said it was for outstanding service in the Hungarian Army.

Later, somewhere, the train stops. My father keeps observing the outside, then falls silent. I realize how pale he is when he turns towards me.

"Don't you feel well?" I ask.

"I feel poorly," he replies. He has never allowed me to see weakness in him before. It scares me almost more than anything I have been through in the last days.

Much later the train slows, and he pulls himself up from the bundle spread out on the floor, looks through the hole again and remarks, "It is not too bad. I see white wooden houses with gardens in front of them."

The next thing I am aware of is an undecipherable language; screaming, yelling, running, unintelligible noises come in from outside. We can't imagine the reason. I get on my feet holding my little daughter tightly. We wait in the now semi-dark boxcar. I glance at my father a few times during the nervous turmoil in the car. Everybody is standing up. At last I notice that some colour is coming back into his face. That is the last time I will ever look at my father's beloved face.

All of a sudden the door bursts open. Men in striped pyjamas jump in, yelling, "Out! Out! Out! Don't take anything. We'll take out everything for you." One of them says to me, "Has the child a grandmother? Give her to the grandmother. Children and grandmothers will be together." I press my daughter closer to my body.

We all climb off the boxcar. One old man is left lying on the floor, too weak to get up. The striped-uniform man yells, "Leave him. Leave him, we'll take care of him."

These men in striped uniforms—I can't see who they are—are busy running, yelling, throwing our pathetic belongings on to the ground in a heap. Mine, tied into a bundle in my mother's light-blue best damask tablecloth, used only for special occasions, goes onto the pile with the rest.

The SS are everywhere. They are stiffly military; stomachs sucked in, heads held high, clubs grasped casually in hand, occasionally hitting their highly polished boots. With difficulty they keep their aggressive, impatient German shepherds at heel. They believe totally in their own superiority, and in their present task. Their machinery is functioning with perfection, down to the pettiest detail. Theirs is a great victory; we are completely defeated.

Stumbling from the boxcar we become dizzy from the sudden daylight, the fresh air and the lack of nourishment. All the striped-uniform men passing by ask me, "Has the child a grandmother?" I hold Kati in my arms until my father takes my daughter and gives her to my mother. From somewhere a rumour has spread; he must have heard it: Grandmothers do not have to work. They will take care of the children.

We are pushed quickly towards a gate. An SS officer is standing there. I get to the gate first, while my mother, holding my daughter, walks behind me. As the SS motions me to the right I hear my mother saying, "Sie ist meine Tochter." I turn. It hurts me that the SS doesn't consider my mother worthy enough to be answered. He motions her gruffly to the left. I march on in the belief that I am sacrificing myself for my mother.

We are pushed into a row of five women, all of us young. From time to time we are ordered to shuffle a few yards forward. We lack the will to lift our eyes from the grey, dust-covered road. Voices come to us from behind the electric wire fences. "Do you have anything to eat?" The voices belong to women with shaved heads, clad in dirty rags, with bits of shoes on their thin, bare feet. They shout to us over and over. Poor women. They must be insane.

I lift my eyes to look at the person next to me. She looks back at me. Our gazes meet and we recognize each other. We haven't met since the trip to Italy. An old school friend. We grasp and squeeze each other's hands. No words are exchanged, only a look of mutual pain.

As we move ahead, lined up five abreast, I catch a glimpse of my mother, her sister, and my grandmother, all standing in a circle together, close to a brick building. My little Kati is skipping joyfully around them, happy to be out of the boxcar at last.

A German guard commands us to move on. A young man drags himself past us, bleeding horribly. He is chased like a wild beast by snapping dogs and by the club-wielding SS. My friend and I exchange a terrified glance. We are silent. We can't do anything for him so we just move on with the others. More women are lined up behind us. I can't see any end to the rows of women. We are hundreds and hundreds now. Trapped.

Abruptly, as I can see only a few rows ahead, I find myself in front of an open door. I step, blinded by the afternoon sun, into a large enclosed hall. Many women are inside already. I want to turn around to orient myself, to see, but I am pushed around, powerless, amid SS shouting and dogs barking. The noise is confusing and terrifying. All around the walls the SS are standing with weapons ready. At the front a woman faces us, and in broken Hungarian she bawls through a bullhorn. "Take your clothes off. Put everything next to you on the floor. You'll be deloused and disinfected."

I turn to my friend next to me. Alarmed, I realize I have lost her in the tumult. I know it will be impossible to find her again. The woman beside me has already started to undress. Slowly, I start to loosen my clothes, looking at all the soldiers, unable to believe they can really mean it.

Everybody ties their clothes together and puts them on the floor. I do, too. Before tying my coat sleeves I take a small snapshot out of my pocket: my little Kati, crouching down between the flowers in my parents' garden. I have a long look at it before I put the photo back, thinking I will pick it up later.

We are all pushed, screamed at, and beaten into a single line. Women sitting with clippers in hand scream, "Move your feet apart!" "Keep your arms up!" "Bend your head down!" My hair falls in a heap on the floor. I stare down at it. "Move, move, move, you animal!"

We are herded into a large concrete room. Rows and rows of showerheads protrude from the ceiling. The doors shut behind us and water sprays down on us for one or two minutes, then stops. The doors open. Kicking and pushing, our captors scream, "Rush, rush, rush! Out, out, you idiots." In a corridor along the wall, women throw old clothes at us. An old black rag hits me. I look at it, surprised. A woman kicks me away, shouting, "Walk, you animal." With difficulty I pull the long-used rag onto my still-wet body. Next, with a house-painter's brush a yellow cross is painted with oil paint down the length of the rag.

35

The terrorizing screaming, yelling and pushing is incessant. As we are herded out again in front of the building, we are knocked into a row of five. I look at the unrecognizable, dehumanized creatures around me. Even sisters don't recognize each other now.

Grey dust lifts as we move our demoralized heavy feet forward. I look to the ground. After what seems like an endless march, we stop at a long barracks with an open latrine along one side. We are kicked and hit through the narrow door, as if it were vital that all eight hundred women get inside instantly. Once inside, we stand waiting in the hot, crowded room that is the barracks. Along with hundreds of others, we have been shaved, stripped of our womanly shape and our dignity in a matter of hours.

A hoarse shouting silences everyone. I can't actually see her through the endless rows of women, but I hear a woman's crude screaming in broken Hungarian coming from the front. Somewhat relieved that we speak a common language, I expect a few soothing words.

"You know where you are?" she yells. "You are in Birkenau-Auschwitz. No one has ever gone out from this place alive. You will all croak here. Ladies and misses don't exist here. There are no dining rooms, no bedrooms, no bathrooms, no running water. The latrines are outside. Don't dare use them before morning. If you dare to go out after dark you'll be shot dead. Sit down where you are. You sleep where you are. There is no supper. Sit down, you imbeciles."

Bewildered, we wonder where to put ourselves while her frenzy of screaming abuse continues. We try desperately to find a place to sit where there is really only room to stand. We all try to squeeze into an impossible space. There is no room, but somehow I manage to kneel and squeeze my feet under me. I close my eyes while it is getting darker and fold my hands for my evening prayer, as I have done every night of my life. I begin to murmur my first intimate words, "My God, King in heaven. . . ." There, I stop. I take my hands apart. Resolutely. I have reached a watershed. I have lost my faith. I feel I will never pray again.

In the dark, our aching, tired limbs slump uncontrolled over those closest to us on the floor. Accompanied by ominous background noises from a concealed world, all eight hundred women collapse in a communal nightmare. From time to time I wake in anguish, frightened by the shape of the mass of bodies. I can hardly remember how I got here. Drifting back to my half-sleep, I long for safety and repose, only to be awakened, still in darkness, to a menacing shout: "Out, out, out, imbecile animals. Move faster!" With a stick in her hand, a woman is shouting. Everybody elbows towards the door in a vain attempt to avoid her blows.

At about four in the morning it is still shivering cold outside, though it is the end of spring. The only visible light comes from the high watchtowers. From the towers, the reflectors constantly scan beyond the borders of the high-voltage wire fence in which we are enclosed. The air smells different from anything I know. Tall chimneys in the distance belch smoke into the air.

"If you dare to move I'll kill you," threatens yet another voice as we are pushed into rows of five along the side of the barracks. We feel very cold and try to keep close to each other for warmth. Having nothing to say, we are silent. Without wanting to, I close my eyes while standing in the row. When I wake from my trance, tears are running down my face.

The morning gets lighter and the woman with the stick gets busier, walking constantly now up and down, brandishing her weapon, shouting and swearing relentlessly. From somewhere, it trickles in to us that the ferociously screaming women are SS helpers. Later we learn they are called *kapos*. In the light of dawn I realize that we are lined up facing the latrine, which is a plank as long as the barracks with holes in it. Under every hole there is a pail. The barracks parallel to ours uses it, and they apparently feel no embarrassment being

37

out in the open this way. I am happy I have no need, having eaten nothing for several days.

Now the vast, barren place in which we have been dumped unfolds in its ugliness. Everything is evil-looking. There are barracks after barracks, but no trees. Not a single one. Not even a blade of grass. Nothing can prosper here. Only hatred. Hairless, sexless women move about a short distance from us. Have we been made purposely despicable so we will be easy to kill? We are repulsive. Were we ever alluring and beautiful?

From different barracks they come, dragging grey blankets through the dust and mud. Oh God! I can see distinctly grey stick-like feet hanging out. They are hauling corpses. Maybe they are forced to remove and discard their dead comrades although they themselves can hardly move.

The sun comes out at last. We guess it must be around ten or eleven in the morning. A kettle appears from somewhere. A big pot with light brownish liquid in it is handed to me by the woman in front of me. I have to drink one sip of it, like everybody else, and then hand it to the woman behind me. The *kapo* bellows instructions from the front of the row. When that is gone, a pot with thick grey feed comes. When the cooking pot reaches me I lift it reluctantly to my lips, not recognizing what it is. The one gulp that I am supposed to lap up flows with difficulty into my mouth. I spit out pieces of black coal along with hard stones. Some time later a chunk of what looks like a piece of broken brick dipped in sawdust—the bread—gets to me. I cannot come to terms with my present state. I throw mine away.

The SS arrive soon after, men and women engaged in relaxed conversation, obviously in the best of moods. Pedantically clean, crisp, perfumed and very sure of themselves, they count us over and over again, dragging it out as though they enjoyed it. We stand in the blazing sun the whole day. By the end of our first day in Auschwitz, many of us are badly burned and covered with blisters.

Our routine is set. We are left to languish, parched and starved, on the barracks floor or outside in the mud, or under the summer heat and dust. We have nothing else to do. With no work, nothing to think about, we languish in purposelessness. And the infernal military machinery does its work day and night. One can be hit any time without warning. Women are selected from our midst, thrown naked onto trucks and taken away. Easily, like potato sacks. We witness the diabetics die in agony for lack of a drop of insulin. The days are contrived for torment.

Sometimes, news trickles in from beyond the barbed wire. But who knows how much is the truth? Stories go from mouth to mouth: "I heard there has been an attempt on Hitler." Another time, the alarms sound in Auschwitz. "The Americans are trying to bombard Auschwitz," is the story. I think to myself, They have better things to do. Another favourite is: "Children are with their grandmothers." In my desperate hope I believe it. One day I hear that pregnant women in the barracks will be transported to a part of the camp where the grandmothers and children are. I scratch a few words on a piece of trash paper to send with one of the women, begging her to look up my dear mother and child. Sending a sign of life is all I can do to assure them that I am not too far away.

We hear news like: "No more cities from Hungary are allowed to deport Jews. We were the last." As much as I want to believe it I doubt the sudden change of heart. In general my own reaction is: And what if it is true? What then?

––––––

"Lager Sperre! Lager Sperre!" (Lock up the barracks! Lock up the barracks!) howls the *kapo*. For no apparent reason, we often spend days or parts of days locked in. We think it is one of the senseless caprices of the SS. But really, it doesn't matter to us where we are.

On one such day, I sit on the floor inside the barracks, half-awake, half-hallucinating as I often am from weakness or depression. Against all odds, a feeling infects me that my friends from Pécs have arrived. Whatever happens I have to get outside and see for myself. I step over people's feet, heading for the door, and manage to get out of the barracks and out of the quarantine area, sliding between barracks until I come to a huge field devoid of buildings. There the hard, stamped yellow clay is crowded with a mass of women in rags. Their scalps are freshly shorn, white. I take my arms out of my long black winter dress and tie it around my waist. The sun is piercing hot; it must be midday. With pain in my heart I begin to whistle as I get closer the melody of "Regen Tropfe" (Rain Drops), our signal between friends from back home. I whistle it a few times and then, unbelievably, the answer comes in the form of another part of the song: "Beim andern Fenster klopfen" (Tap at another window). We both keep whistling and going in the direction of the sound, while searching among the unrecognizably transformed women. At last we spot each other. With breaking heart, which they do not notice, I hug my dear friends from Pécs, Hanna and Eszter.

They greet me as if they were expecting me to welcome them to the camp. Hanna's first words are: "My sister fell unconscious on the wagon floor and the striped-uniform man didn't let me take her. He said she'll be taken to the hospital."

Eszter gazes at my appearance with some distaste: "How come you are so unkept?" They both ask for water. Only then do I realize that after the terrible shock of the trip, the heat and the lack of water, they are confused and not able to grasp yet where they are. As I couldn't grasp it totally for weeks after my arrival. In their dazed state they look upon me as a hostess in my own home, as it was when we last saw each other. I promise to bring them water, though I know perfectly well there is none. The only water we have arrives in a truck every few days—a single barrel with one tap for thousands of women. I never go for water. It is useless. But most of the women are desperate and risk a ferocious fight and a clubbing from the SS to get to the water when it arrives, only to walk away without any, in tears. The barrel empties in minutes and there is nowhere to go for more.

I run blindly and I find a puddle. I dip my dress into the muddy hole and run back to my friends as fast as I can. Next to them is a woman I recognize, an elegant, beautiful woman when I last saw her. She is half-leaning with one elbow on the ground. Her eyes are closed, but her lips are moving as though she were trying to say something. No sound comes. I squeeze a few drops onto her lips, too. Women begin to encircle me, hoping for a drop of water. I run again and again to the puddle.

And then on one of my trips to the puddle I stop. What am I doing? What do I imagine I am? I have nothing here. I am nobody here. The sudden rekindling of my dormant instinct to be useful is of no avail. For a short moment I have been human again, but the reality is that I am helpless to make any difference to their further existence. My spirit and my will to exist ebb away. I sneak back into the barracks, risking punishment. The last hours' experience, seeing the many familiar and loved faces on the threshold of peril, leaves me both emotionally and physically drained.

After that initial meeting with Hanna and Eszter, days go by, maybe weeks. I know my friends must be in some barracks close by, but in my deep lethargy I can't summon enough strength even to look for them. I drag myself out to the endless roll calls or to the sadistic punishments we get in the "B" lager where I am like a useless parasite and where, to beat the pain, I sometimes escape into dreams. We are often made to kneel on the dirt road, knees bare, our arms straight up in the air, sometimes holding a stone. While kneeling this way, half aware, half dreaming, I hear my Kati's voice call "Mummy." I move to run to her when I am dizzied by a blinding lash into my right eye from somewhere behind me. Disoriented, jolted out of a dream,

41

I can't grasp why I got hurt. I can't see any wrongdoing on my part that deserved such punishment. At first I believe I have lost my right eye.

Then the blow acts as a catalyst. It is as if I haven't been aware until now of where I am. Understanding comes to me suddenly: my deeds, good or bad, don't matter. I am unwanted either way. My existence is extinguishable at any moment, without anybody's regret. I am here under the sway of unchecked hatred, delivered to sadists, protected neither by country nor by law.

Number 168

I notice one day through my apathy the new faces that were driven into our barracks by the SS. I discover Hanna and Eszter among them. We are weak, incapable of emotions, but we register some comfort that at last we are together in the same barracks.

The *kapo* is excitedly running up and down; it leads us to guess that something is ahead, although by now we are largely indifferent to the future. She chases us into rows of five, indulging even more than usual in her insults, and lets us stand for hours under the hot sun. At last she screams, "QUIET!" and it seems the hot air comes to a fearful stand-still. Dr. Mengele and his staff arrive. He looks deadly serious and infallible, as though the outcome of the war depended on his enterprise. The ubiquitous stick hits his high polished boot. Next to him, with pencil and writing block, is his red-haired secretary and another beautiful, high-ranking SS woman caressing a small lap dog. If only they had a grain of humour or self-criticism they would know what laughable imbeciles they are. But unfortunately they possess only brutish strength and we are in their hands. No one dares to breathe.

An SS woman howls, "Take your clothes off. Hold them high over your heads and move by in single file." We walk by in a single file in front of Mengele. One look of his well-practised eye is enough to send some of us right, some to the left with a sure single crisp point of his stick. Then he goes on hitting his boot. I don't care to which side I am sent. Which side is condemned to live? Which side is finished now?

When the selection is over, a group of us find ourselves together. With me are a cousin, a schoolfriend, Hanna and Eszter, along with about seven hundred other women. They let us put our rags on and make us march away immediately. After a long walk we find ourselves again in a place where showerheads spray water down from the ceiling. Our clothing is changed. We also get underwear, and though it is mostly soiled it seems disinfected at least. This time I receive a short-sleeved summer dress. The yellow cross is again painted the length of my back and I get distinguished from the nameless trash by a disc stamped *Häftling 168* (Convict 168) hung around my neck. After the shower we are herded into an oversized, all-concrete washroom. The concrete floor has a sharp slant toward the middle. Here I squat on the slanted cold floor in a state of total apathy, until later in the evening when my name echoes through the washroom, going from mouth to mouth until it finds its way to me. I can hardly believe it. I ask cautiously: "You mean me?" and I find myself meeting a woman who is actually clean and decently dressed.

"I bring you a message from your cousin Ditta," she says. I gasp. "She asked me to find you," she explains. At this point we are encircled by women who have become aware of something unusual and, like myself, are either eager to learn directly about our environs or hope to meet this person who may have come to help. (Each of us thinks, Maybe she will sneak a piece of bread to me.) But mostly, we pray for a positive answer to the frightening question that all of us secretly ask: Is there a way out of here?

The woman goes on: "Ditta couldn't come herself because she just went on her night shift."

"Is there work here?" I ask.

"She works in the Kanada Kommando."

"What is the Kanada Kommando?" I ask.

"It's where women sort out what you people bring with you to Auschwitz. Maybe you've seen them. They all wear a red kerchief."

"Perhaps they did pass us once. I heard them singing, leaving a cloud of perfume behind."

"They do pour the bottles of perfume out, or on themselves," she says, "to try to make things useless to Germans. They also cut fur coats and other stuff into bits and pieces if they have a chance."

I think how lucky they are to be able to act on their own will. It also eases my thoughts about Ditta that she is relatively well. I ask her: "What do you think will happen to us?" She thinks we are selected for work. I am not sure whether she knows this or says it out of kindness. I think to send a few words to Ditta. The woman assures me she will give a message to her and lends me her pencil. One of the women readily gives me a piece of her crushed brown paper to write on. I want to ask Ditta mainly about the children, whether she knows where they are.

After the woman leaves, a forgotten feeling comes over me. It is like a miracle that I have been singled out with a personal message in this godforsaken, unholy place. Maybe from now on everything will change for the better. The fact that Ditta is here and contact was possible is like a message from a normal world. It gives me hope that my child, my parents and my brother are also somewhere here and that I will be able to hear from them.

We spend the night on the slanted concrete floor, in our clothes, as always. The next day we fill the boxcars of a freight train. We don't know which part of diabolical Auschwitz we are going to, neither do we know what time of day it is. We do know the date. It is August 28, 1944.

The train goes into motion, carrying us away again. I am standing on the moving train at the half-open sliding door. As the train slowly gathers speed, as I leave this hell, this evil place where I arrived together with my loved ones, my heart feels heavier and heavier. Where should I picture them? Is a distance growing between us as I am taken further and further away? I don't want to go.

I stand there while the door is still open, to watch through the opening the barren yellow soil and the grey barracks falling behind us. The freshness of limitless green meadows lies ahead, like cleanliness after decay. That means life still exists beyond the electric wires, that other people continue their lives normally, undisturbed. It is hard to picture it. The grass, the trees, the various greens, the billowy cornfields, the fenceless horizon is, to my eyes, like crystal-clear spring water to the wanderer in an arid desert. I long to drink it up.

Soon after, the train stops and we are locked away from the outside. Hanna and Eszter make room for me on the floor next to them. One has to muster one's energy when it is needed. Strength is what counts to fight for advantages as small as a place to sit. From such victories comes survival. They can make a whole world of difference because our lives hang on so little. All kinds of coteries are formed from the need for joint power. Thrown into camp and treated as worthless material, one's destiny is quickly sealed, especially as one loses strength and energy. The need for association is so strong that a faint link is enough to build a life-saving relationship and to create instant support. A vague connection will do. "I went to school with your cousin," or, "The street I lived on was not far from your place." Such tenuous links form bridges. Often a weak person would try to endear herself through small services to a stronger one, or perhaps a stronger woman needs an interest to fight for, a weaker person to protect. My strength lies in Hanna and Eszter. Their unselfish friendship, their endless moral support and understanding, are what help me through. And not just once, but many times.

———

First of September, 1944. The freight train stops between a factory building and a few barracks. I stand up. My ears are ringing and the world gets dark. The next sound I hear is Eszter's harsh voice. "We do not play that kind of game here. Pull yourself together." I feel their strong support under my arms. I manage to get off with their help. Many of us are sick, mostly with debilitating diarrhea. We think it is from the long train ride in the summer hot spell.

Once we have disembarked, Hanna, Eszter, my cousin and the schoolfriend do their best to keep the five of us together and, if possible, next to the same five we were with in Auschwitz. I am lucky to be with them, a passive member, drifting uncaringly towards whatever comes next.

On the ground the SS count us endlessly behind the fence in front of the barracks. Some of us can hardly stand. While the counting goes on, girls are secretly holding up the sick, hiding them from the SS. It is hard to believe that what is going on is unnoticed. Maybe the problem is too new for them to deal with immediately. After the roll call we are let into the barracks, counted and commanded into rooms. Thirty-two women in each. My good Hanna and Eszter keep me between them to get me into the same room as them, knowing I am unwilling to wrestle or push people.

In the barracks there are plank bunk beds with straw sacks for mattresses. Each of us gets a grey blanket, handed out by one of our group. The SS don't waste much time finding their best helpers from among our women. They quickly delegate to them certain distribution tasks. Each of us gets a hardware bowl and an iron spoon that we are told we can keep, which means some upgrading in comparison with Auschwitz. Kettles are put up outside with something steaming in them. We form a single line with bowls in hand, and the new helpers measure out ladles of cabbage soup as the SS stand by, smiling. We tell each other that it is cabbage soup, glad to recognize the stuff as food. We are stunned by our unexpected upgrading in Lippstadt, our new camp. We hear people saying we can go for a second bowl if there is any left over.

Our new possessions and the fact that there are only thirty-two of us in a room means we are living in a much better situation. Part of me would like to settle with that thought and not think about the future. But I can't overlook the fact that I am still in my enemy's hands and that my fate is changeable any time. Some decide not to think, others turn to humour. I hear a woman saying, "Girls, I heard that tomorrow the dinner won't be cabbage soup, but mashed potatoes and hot dogs." I am grateful to those people who are capable of jesting in this situation.

We make ready for the night on our bunk beds, hardly able to wait to lie down. They feel luxurious even though the straw is broken into tiny pieces in the mattress, mostly turned into dust. At last, after months, we can actually stretch out to sleep. The lights go off and there is quiet. The next moment we all go crazy as hundreds of bedbugs fall hungrily on us. We scratch and chase them most of the night. It makes me wonder who the slave workers were who occupied our beds before us. And where did they go?

In the early hours of the morning the satiated bedbugs disappear only to be replaced by the shouting of the SS. "Get up, Get up." It is about 4:30 a.m. We are out for the usual lengthy counting process. Actually we don't even mind the fresh air that early after the unbearable heat in the barracks. It is still summer in Westfalen, Germany, about a thousand kilometres west of Hungary, and it doesn't begin to cool off until the end of September. Later, some warm water is ladled into our bowls. I can't call it coffee, but it does settle our raw stomachs.

At 6:00 a.m. the reason for our transfer to Lippstadt becomes apparent. We are led into the munitions factory and our first day at work begins. The heads of the workers already there turn curiously to look at us as we march in. I am very much aware of the surprise we create, we strange creatures. We are like women out of a lunatic asylum, heads shaved, grey, starved faces with sunken dull eyes, worn dresses hanging loosely down on bare legs in ragged shoes. I am also positively aware that the onlookers can't imagine that I am not what they see. I am somebody else, known only to me and my friends.

There are huge machines and smaller ones, all grey, intimidating solid steel. I have never in my life been in a factory, let alone an armament factory. What am I doing here? And what is any one of us doing here? But we can't wonder about that too long because German *Meisters* take us away and lead us to different machines. Eszter and I are taken to a row of drilling machines with ten others. We each get a machine to work on. We are shown how to drill holes in hand grenades, using both hands at the same time. Top turn the hand grenade shell with one hand while pulling down the handle with the other hand to drill the holes. We find out that we have to do this for twelve hours daily. Hanna is at a soldering machine used to finish the hand grenade shells.

Our *Meister* is German, but the foreman turns out to be a young Ukrainian woman. I manage to speak a few words to her while she stands behind me watching the job I do. She is able to say a few German words and from that I put together that she is here on forced labour. (The Germans call it "voluntary.") She lives in a camp with the other voluntary workers and they are free to move about in a limited territory. They are also free to work on nearby farms on their own time. Envious, I think how lucky they are.

After six hours' work, at noon, the signal sounds for a fifteen-minute lunch break. We are told to line up with our bowls at the kettle in the middle of the factory. We receive again a ladle of cabbage soup. During that fifteen minutes we dare to lift our eyes and look around. Also, meeting at the kettle we are able to exchange words with our people from different parts of the factory. We soon learn that the young men in the factory are Italian prisoners with the same freedom as the

Ukrainians. Later, back in the barracks, we exchange our observations from every corner of the factory, depending on where we work, as well as the latest news we manage to overhear about the situation on various German fronts. Whether the news is authentic we can't know, but it helps to nurture our hopes.

In the middle of the first afternoon I am astounded to notice the Ukrainian girl bending down, sneaking a red apple into my lap. The view of that fresh, beautiful healthy red apple brings tears to my eyes. What can she find appealing about me in my state? Later, she hands me a glass of milk, to drink right away, before anyone should see it. I let my locked heart open cautiously to feel for a moment that there is hope. Maybe the whole world has not gone crazy.

At 6:00 p.m. every day the signal sounds, indicating the end of our shift. We rush toward the door to punch out. It is the end of the twelve-hour work day. The long hours of drilling are too hard for our wrists and fingers. We are aching, tired and hungry. As we leave, we glance at the factory entrance. The incoming girls are beginning their night shift, only somewhat more restored than we are. I manage to smuggle my apple out and later share it with Hanna and Eszter. I also share its beautiful story with them. They are as pleased as I am.

We are counted as we pass through the gate into the camp area and then lined in fives and counted again. If the erratic mood of the SS is satisfied we can then go into the barracks. At the door we receive about a third of an ounce of margarine, two teaspoons of molasses, and on good days, one slice of bologna. Inside our rooms are several loaves of bread, each for either seven or nine people, to be cut somehow. Dividing the bread is a huge problem. Whom to trust with the task among the hungry women is quite another. Eventually I am chosen.

Our best short minutes of the day come after the bread is passed out. At last we sit on our bunks with our portions and gnaw them slowly to make the bread last longer. Finishing it is final; nowhere to go for more. It will be a twenty-four-hour wait before we will get solid food again.

Still, after Auschwitz this is luxury. We even have water in the washroom and we can drink when we want, though it is sparse and sometimes dwindles away. But after a while we acquire the skill of using it carefully to clean up at the end of the day.

As soon as we can, we lie down for the night. The lights go off and the bedbugs come to feed, but we are too tired to care. However, a new disturbance arises. Our weakened kidneys can't take the daily cabbage soup, so too often at night we must make our way to the latrine. Day after day, week after week we get nothing but cabbage soup. It is only later, when the trees turn to autumn-yellow and the cabbage soup changes to yellow, too, that we suspect what we are eating. To make it worse, it is made without a pinch of salt, and very often has a chemical Lysol taste. As hungry as we are, it takes willpower or a friend's urging to force it down.

Ever since our first day in Lippstadt, we have heard a blunt pounding in the distance. We hope, without putting much trust in it, that it is the English and American armies shelling the Germans. There are rumours that the pounding comes from Aachen, a German town on the Belgian border about three hundred kilometres away. The pounding accompanies us day and night, but as much as we want it to, it never seems to sound any closer. Bombers also frequently fly over us, raising our hopes. If we happen to be in the factory when they are heard overhead, the SS chase us like madmen with sticks and belts to the barracks, where we are supposed to go into a ridiculously flimsy shelter. Then they run, out of breath, into their concrete bunker. We immediately go back inside the barracks where they can't see us, and pray for a long alarm.

One day it seems as if the bombs are falling practically on the camp. The noise is deafening. It is amplified by the hollow wooden walls of our barracks, which shake like cardboard boxes. We are looking from the ceiling to the walls and back to the ceiling, deciding which direction to jump if anything comes down on us, when we hear my schoolfriend's sleepy voice coming from her top bunk bed: "What is going on? Is there a bombing?" We manage to laugh. The bombs are not what we fear. Every minute of every day is a threat, and that we can't escape. The best we can do is to stretch out on our bunks for a blessed sleep.

———

As the weather slides slowly into winter, our bread portions get smaller. Cutting and dividing the loaves into seven, nine, or later to eleven portions, even more than before, invariably results in a barrage of insults. My group alone, where I am the cutter, has no complaint. Gradually all the dividing is completely given over to me in our room. I only take on this difficult task to silence the unending squabble, which upsets me; my belief in the persuasive power of honesty is unchanged. The dividing is further complicated by various factors. For one thing, the loaves must be divided into uneven numbers of portions. Furthermore, the recipient can't tolerate that the next person might get a sliver more than her. I can easily be accused of partiality.

The knife is a makeshift piece of iron, stolen and secretly sharpened with a grinding wheel in the factory. Usually, while waiting for their portions, everyone stands around the small table watching while I cut. Some, the closer ones, moisten their fingers with their tongues ready in case a crumb falls on the table. One day I hear a woman in the room say: "I was about to pick it up, but it flew away." It was a fly.

———

In grey monotony we grind away our days between barracks and factory with hardly a bright moment. There is some small diversion when the machine needs repair and one of the Italians comes. He does the repairs. He usually asks us, "How long you want to sit on the latrine?" That means that he will play with the machinery as long as he can without being caught by the Germans. Sabotage in a small way.

A few words with the Ukrainian foreman in a mixed language is also a change. One day she appears with a small sack of salt sewed in a cloth and puts it on my lap while I sit at the drilling machine. I can't believe my luck. Salt is the most coveted commodity. It is readily exchangeable, as we lack it badly. I take it back with me, hidden from the SS, and we make a plan to sell it. Eszter is the best businesswoman among us, so she becomes our agent. She sells a teaspoonful of it for a slice of bread. Word goes around fast about our salt; people come with their slices of bread to our bunks, where Eszter keeps her business hours.

The extra nutrition we purchase with the salt lasts us for weeks and does a world of good. Meanwhile the Ukrainian girl tells me one day in pidgin German: "Ik laufen." I don't know whether I really understand what she is saying, but after a few days when I don't see her, I know I did. "I'll run away," she said. She left me with the sack of salt. I keep her kindly in my memory.

Twelve hours a day, six days a week, days one week and nights the next. We live only to work. Our nutrition is balanced in such a way that we will last as long as we are needed. We are replaced if we fall away. After a few months, one hundred and fifty of us have fallen sick and are sent to the closest extermination camp: Bergen-Belsen. They are replaced immediately by Polish Jewish women. It is hard to hold out when all conditions are against us.

Night shift is one of our killers. When it ends at 6:00 a.m., the SS keep us standing outside. Often we can't get to rest before 9:00 a.m. At noon we are awakened to do some useless work around the barracks. At 6:00 p.m. our shift begins again. I find it brutally hard, especially around 3:00 in the morning when I feel as if the life is going out of me. Eszter keeps talking to me, trying to keep me awake. But one night I feel simply at the end of my strength. Unmindful of Eszter's begging, knowing that the foreman will discover me, I sit down among the hand grenades and instantly fall asleep. But not for long. Soon I hear Eszter yelling: "Böske!" I jump up and run to my machine before the foreman can get to me, shaking his iron rod.

I find Saturday even harder than the night shift. We are in the factory eighteen hours between Friday at 6:00 p.m. and Saturday at 6:00 p.m. Then all the machines finally stop till Sunday at 6:00 p.m. (although we are occasionally called to work at six in the morning on Sundays as well). A sudden hollow silence follows. It leaves me with a terrible ringing in my ears, a loss of balance and shattered nerves. I am incapacitated in my movements or am only very slowly, and with great effort, able to move my arms and hands. It takes a few hours to recuperate.

After the exhausting night shift, Sunday, if we are lucky, is supposed to be free. If there is enough water we have a chance to really wash up—although always in cold water, summer or winter. We disregard the glassless windows, or the broken ones. We don't care anymore about the SS guards walking up and down in front of them. We just undress as if they weren't there. We know they don't consider us to be humans anyway.

———

While we engage in our ultimate physical struggle, our non-physical needs are totally dormant, but they come to the surface instantly after just a little rest. As soon as we sit among our fellows, our old selves pop up obediently and our minds travel away from our wretched existence. We often have long conversations with Hanna and very often, to the whole room's delight, she recalls poems. Then everybody who wants to leave the present behind listens quietly, remembering a nobler world in the past. She recites from the work of poets we always felt and feel akin to, like François Villon, Paul Geraldi, Faludi, Adi Endre. The pure, unburdened love for art replaces somewhat, without our awareness, our true longings.

Sometimes she sings, saving our sensibilities from oblivion. Her warm speaking voice adapts itself smoothly to both arts. When people get to know about her talent, she gets invited often to other rooms. She also draws in our room, lacking paper, on the walls. She finds charcoal to draw with in the rubbish outside.

We also have some short conversations with fellow prisoners which, in some ways, include the past, but don't step over neutral ground. Intuitively avoiding painful points by exchanging recipes fits neutrality perfectly. Giving or listening to recipes takes a different shape and deeper meaning here than it had when we were free. It serves an unusual double purpose. First, the recipe and its quality throws some light on each person's previous circumstances; also, remembering the past in this way lends new energy to the owner of the recipe. The other advantage is that the listener raises her spirits by imagining a merry, beautiful home where the recipe can be made. Maybe it awakes a tiny secret hope. The colourful picture takes us away from our dull existence for a short while. In the same vein are the dreams of crystal and porcelain that I entertain while I drill the monotonous grey hand grenades.

In the middle of winter, all of a sudden, unbelievable words circulate. We are to get winter coats. Sure enough, women line up for coats after work in front of the SS office. They stand in line, barely minding the beating that goes with every coat. They wait for hours, for weeks on end. The coats are used and flimsy, but they provide an extra layer for an emaciated body in the cold. The SS could hand them out in one afternoon, but they choose another way. The price for every coat is a beating. I refuse to stand in line like a beggar, to ask for a coat. I refuse to submit myself to their sadism, to heighten their imagined superiority with every wicked blow. I decide that although they can get everything else from me by force, including my life, they won't get my pride. I won't go for a coat. I stand outside during the endless counting each morning at 5:00 a.m. and each evening after 6:00 p.m. Thick snow accumulates on my back, on my short-sleeved summer dress, on my bare feet covered only in wooden clogs. Hanna and Eszter urge me to go for a coat. The constant question, "Aren't you cold?" annoys me. Their steady queries are met with a curt, unexplained "No." I am the only person in the camp without a coat.

As we are about to go in for the night shift one day, an SS unexpectedly pulls me out of the line, takes me into his office and throws a coat at me. No beating. It is a grey coat. The inside is blood spattered and on the lining is handwritten in ink a woman's name and the name of her city, Riga. I think about the woman who owned it once and wonder about her fate. In the end I refuse to wear it. Hanna and Eszter take the coat without my knowledge, throw the lining out, wash the coat with difficulty in the little cold water we have, and re-model it with stolen thread. They do all this at night, after their daily shift. Having done all that, they still have enough patience to coax me into wearing it. I wish my friends hadn't put so much care and work into it. I would rather take a beating from the SS for defiance than wear it, but that would be inconsiderate. So I put it on reluctantly, holding myself away from the coat stiffly. It never really becomes mine.

In the meantime we are growing weaker, hungrier and colder in the winter of 1944-45, the coldest to hit Europe in decades. We promise ourselves every evening to put away at least a small bite of our bread portion for the next day, but we can't keep our promise. We are just too hungry. Then Hanna comes with the news that she has been offered an extra portion of soup for each of us if we undertake to carry the daily coffee kettle at four in the morning. We take the offer gladly, even if it means an earlier wake-up time. Thanks to Hanna's popularity, we get this privileged job. We keep it for two months, until some of the girls begin to hate us. Then to give others a chance, we step aside.

One Sunday in 1945 we are marched to downtown Lippstadt after a bombardment to carry rubble and clean up houses. This is the first time we have stepped outside the camp's fence into an urban area with a civilian population. It is the first time we are able to glance at the city where we have already spent months. Aside from some bombed-out buildings, I am astonished to see that life goes on, apparently undisturbed. Germans live as if nothing happened. Well-fed children are dressed for winter. People in luxurious fur coats go about their business. Indifferent, unimpressed by us tattered, starved women, they don't give a damn. They seem convinced that they are in their rightful position and we deserve to be where we are. It seems that the pounding from Aachen won't come in time. That night, back in the barracks, I lie down, thinking I never want to get up again.

From the Ashes

It is Easter Sunday, April 1945, early in the morning, maybe just dawn. We stand still, like frozen grey statues. Us. Seven hundred and thirty women, wrapped in wet, grey, threadbare blankets, standing in the rain. Our blankets hang over our heads, drape down to the soil. We hold them closed with our hands from the inside, leaving only a small opening to peer out, so that we save the precious warmth of our breath. Who knows why we are here. The SS drove us out of the barracks one morning without explanation. "OUT! OUT!" was all we heard. Getting out didn't take too long since we had no belongings to pack, except for the blanket, some oily rags if we managed to steal them from the factory, a few nails and some pieces of string. I also have a nail that I'd filed down, for cleaning my fingernails (clean fingernails had become my obsession), and a piece of broken comb I had traded for a slice of bread. We hid our meagre possessions just in case, like squirrels who bury trifles for some time later.

They made us line up in the usual row of five, counted us and shouted, "LOS! LOS!" (Get out! get out!) We marched off. Herded like beasts, we were marching toward Bergen-Belsen, the extermination camp, the final point of our existence.

Three days on the road, and here we stand in the rain, in the middle of a field, between the stumps of last summer's corn stalks, now turned to mush. The soil hasn't yet been able to absorb all the melted snow of the cruel winter of 1944-45. Standing there, we remain motionless for who knows how long, daring no question, expecting no answer, knowing no time.

Sometime later I vaguely hear someone saying, "I noticed the SS took his Hitler picture from his pocket, crumbled it into small pieces and threw it away."

I think to myself that this must be a rumour like hundreds I have heard before. And even if it is true, they are still armed. And why would anyone save us? Who can tell what is the limit of their irrational hate? I don't believe in their clemency. Unwilling to let myself entertain useless hope, I vacate my mind of further thoughts and return to my familiar indifferent, animal-like state. More time goes by. We remain in the same spot, waiting for nothing. We know well that there is no one to ask. Only the SS know what lies ahead.

Later, it could be hours or minutes, I notice a woman not far from me, pointing to something in the distance. Suddenly she cries out in a muffled voice, "Oh, God, is it possible that I see a house with a white flag hanging out the window? Does that mean surrender?"

Her words spread quickly. Grey blankets slowly begin to move. First they are apprehensively pushed aside and eyes peer out. Then, when more flags appear in the distance on a cluster of houses, we become gradually convinced that something unusual is happening. We turn our eyes, still veiled by a shadow of doubt, toward the edge of the wooded area where the SS are. But they are not there. They are nowhere. Like ghosts, the SS and their dogs have vanished into thin air. Without a sound.

A hollow moment devoid of feeling or understanding holds us inert and confused. Is this the miracle we have hoped for without ever believing in it? Is this the phenomenon called freedom that has unexpectedly arrived? Is it reality or a dream?

Shaking and shivering wretchedly from freedom's first sudden brush, we free our hands to reach to heaven and fall down to share our boundless relief with the one divinity, the Earth. Hugging the wet soil, in a foe's alien land, our long-arrested pain breaks loose in tearless lumps of sobs that lie abandoned on the cold hostile ground.

The sound of distant roaring jerks us back to our feet. We listen, not knowing what to expect. The roaring approaches closer and closer. Then, in only a moment, on the main road, tanks begin to appear one after another from behind the trees. A white star is marked on each one.

"The Americans! The Americans!" we scream. We all run toward the tanks as fast as we can, as fast as our limited strength and our wooden clogs will allow us.

Thunder engulfs us. Strange prehistoric creatures move by, and with uninterrupted persistence push forward, like a mirage, making the road under our feet vibrate as we stand on the roadside watching. After the tanks come the fast-moving military trucks. Healthy young American GIs stand on the tops like statues of Victory. The view of them brings us hope. At first they seem surprised to see us along the roadside. Then, by impulse, they begin to empty their pockets, throwing whatever they find down to us, along with anything else at hand in the trucks. They smile kindly, waving to us as they speed by, tossing chocolates, cigarettes and gum into the air.

I catch one of those beautiful packages, gilded and sealed in foil. I hold it carefully in my hand and admire its perfection. I see in it a message from an ideal world, put together with care, especially for me. I can't understand the words written on it but I put it into my pocket with care and much anticipation. Later, when after several attempts I can't eat it, I try to decipher the writing on it again and discover the international word, "tobacco." I consult my friends and we decide that what I have been trying to eat is chewing tobacco.

Most of us watch, captivated, as the Americans pass by, but not Eva the Dancer. We have called her that because we never learned her family name. She knows how to leave bad memories quickly behind, how to get on with life anew. While the rest of us stare in disbelief at the tanks and the trucks, we notice her being pulled up onto one of the slower-moving trucks by two GIs.

Then I remember the first time I saw her, on the long ride in the locked boxcar from Auschwitz to somewhere. The boxcar was filled to more than capacity, and then hermetically sealed. Our only possession was about eight ounces of bread for the entire trip. We simply sat on the floor in our rags, with our heads shaved, exhausted, hardly surviving the summer heat, holding our bread in our hands, because there was nowhere else to keep it. I noticed a girl crawling about our feet with a box of two hundred German cigarettes. She offered one to each of us. More accurately she forced one on each of us. Anybody who dared refuse to take a cigarette was met with an avalanche of obscenities.

Though I never actually exchanged a word with her, I felt close to her for that first unselfish gesture, and thankful to her for the moments in the barracks when she was able to help us out of our misery.

Occasionally, on winter evenings, when some life was left in us after the twelve-hour shift, we would sit on our straw sacks, with only the moon's reflection off the snow for light, and in the semi-dark we could discern her small hungry face, her round, astonished eyes, the line of her free-standing ears, and the shadow of her cropped hair. We listened and were transported by her stories.

All of us became lost in her memories, in our dreams, forgetting ourselves as we were swept into her tales about Egypt. There she had been a dancer and a cabaret singer. We followed her into that glorious colourful life, into the streets of lazy, torpid, exotic Cairo where "heads turned when I passed by in my long, white ermine cape, graciously holding my two splendid white Afghan hounds on their extended leash." Her abrupt change of fortune only occurred because she gave in to her longing to see her native Hungary again in 1944. The Germans caught up with her there.

It seems somehow fitting that in the very first hour of our liberation she mounts that American truck, never to be seen again.

The passage of the army dries up after a while, and the rumble with it. In the silence we become aware of ourselves. Some of us are bewildered, some more composed, and many nervously search the terrain with apprehensive eyes. There is no limit, no wire fence. We are overwhelmed by freedom's first problem—that one can make one's own decisions. After a few undecided worried looks, half steps, and turns in all directions, most women run, picking up speed, toward the houses. We decide to follow, Hanna, Eszter and I. We try to question some runners who we think can spare a second in the excitement and know more than we do, but only a few unclear words fly back to us in response. We see that nobody knows anything.

As we head for the village, a girl comes running, wildly gesticulating, shouting that she knows where the SS supply cart is, because she was pushing it when they disappeared. There is bread and other food on it, but she needs help.

We recognize a great opportunity to get something to eat, and join her at the cart a few kilometres back. We eat some of the bread, as much as our shrunken stomachs can take, and then struggle to push and pull the cart towards the village. When we arrive there we are immediately surrounded by girls claiming its contents. "This is ours, too," they argue, while picking the cart empty. Not even outraged, we walk away, leaving the empty cart behind in the middle of the road.

We three, Hanna, Eszter and I, find ourselves in a town we never planned to see. Abruptly released, devoid of identity, we walk dazedly down its main street. We stumble, puzzled and vulnerable in our mortal foe's town, hoping secretly, if they are watching, for some understanding. We are like children marvelling over something, seeing it for the first time—and seeing ourselves for the first time, too. The further we go, the more we want to see. We want to see behind the closed doors, behind the snow-white ruffled curtains covering the sparkling windows. We want to see into the church with its kneeling worshippers, inside the schoolyard with children playing, the conscientious people who take care of the flowers in the front yards. We want to know what they think when they see us. Who prays in the church? Whose children go to school? Who lives in the meticulous houses? But no one is about. Not a soul is out. Insecure? Or too proud? But we are proud, too, Hanna, Eszter and me. We know without saying it that each of us remembers the civilized background in which our friendships started. This background obliges us to act in a civilized manner, even under the present boundless, anarchic conditions.

As we trudge to the middle of the town, we come to a two-storey building. *Gasthaus* is written on it. I presume they have a washroom, and decide spontaneously to go there. Though I am frightened, I finally put my hand on the doorknob and open it. Then I stop. Normal, healthy-looking people are at the tables, eating their meals. At first it is inconceivable. Maybe the uncertainty of the surrender made them flock here, all so well dressed. Not knowing what else to do, I go up to the person at the counter and ask, in her own language, where the washroom is. She points to the corridor. I cross the room uneasily, aware that I am being followed by stiff, frozen glances. They seem to be saying, "How does she dare?" but I can't do anything except stiffen my shoulders and march through.

On my way out of the washroom I pass the kitchen and I step in because the door is open and no one is inside. I look around and notice a big pot on the counter. I haven't seen a pot in a kitchen for such a long time. When I bend over it, the intoxicating aroma of fresh milk rises up like a drug. On impulse I just pick up the entire pot and take it with me, leaving by the back door. I hurry around to the street, where my friends are waiting for information about my first washroom. My brazen action triggers a cold dizzy shiver through me. Is it me who did that?

Seeing me coming back with the big pot, my friends ask, "What's that?" We all drink the milk straight from the pot.

Later we three sit on the street corner for a while just watching the unusual bustle. We sit there as an audience, unable to take up a role yet, but admiring those who can. Girls are running from house to house in their unkempt greasy overalls and wooden clogs. Some are carrying arms full of goods, mostly clothes, and some have impatiently pulled dresses right over their dirty outfits. We see expensive furs flung on top of oil-drenched overalls.

Then we look into houses where the most audacious girls have already settled. Finding the doors open, they have simply walked in. They discover the food warming on stoves, and the tables set for the festive Easter meal. Assuming the owners have gone into last-minute hiding close by, the girls simply lock the doors from inside so no one else—not even others from our group—can intrude, and make themselves at home. As we linger watching, we see one group having a relaxed bath in the middle of someone's kitchen, in the washing trough which they found somewhere around the house.

Eventually my two friends and I find ourselves back on the same highway where we saw the American tanks. We are surprised to discover that we are not alone. Other prisoners of different origins are also on the streets, emerging from somewhere, heading somewhere, without any fixed goal. Wearing dirty grey pieces of cloth, they are dragging their tired feet in ill-fitting clogs. They smile, and we respond with the knowing smile of solidarity. And we all stop as if for a long conversation. But we say aloud only the two words, "DEUTSCHLAND KAPUTT!" And they answer, "DEUTSCHLAND KAPUTT!" Because we all speak different languages. We don't understand each other. We say goodbye, a ready smile on our lips, but our eyes are not so ready. The chased, hungry, bewildered look has not disappeared.

We meet others. We wave and shout over the road, already more relaxed, in chummy closeness, "DEUTSCHLAND KAPUTT!" We repeat it over and over again to ex-prisoners on the move. Often we return the Russian salute, "Zdravstrvuite," which we learn instantly. All these people, like us, have been dumped here from every corner of Europe, speaking only their own tongue. Our communication with them is sign language or the few broken German words we have all picked up in the camps. But for now "DEUTSCHLAND KAPUTT!" is enough. It says it all.

I find that, while outwardly we three don't look any different from any of those we meet, I feel we have remained richer. I believe we managed to salvage our souls. We kept our trust and our friendship, which helped us to keep our hope. Hatred couldn't harden us.

We take lightly the American patrol's warning, "The front is not secure yet. The Germans can still come back." After not even a full day of freedom, we don't believe that it would be possible. Even to think about it is unlikely after we just gained back our lives. Could fate possibly repeat itself a second time? Rerun the same bad play? It looks as if I am not alone in my belief, as nobody is willing to stop doing what they are about to do and prepare for the possibility of a German retaliation.

As the day passes, we look for accommodation, and by opening an unlocked door facing the sidewalk, we chance upon a place that is perfectly appropriate. It is a large empty hall with a stage at one end that looks as if it might have been a cultural meeting centre for Nazis. We move in with seven other girls, making ten. Our two rows of five from camp are kept intact. We feel more comfortable with each other than with any others.

Leaving the door ajar, we search for a corner to lie down. Habit dictates that our whole group is within reach. The cover is our grey blanket and anyone who has stolen oil rags rolls them up for a pillow. Locking the door doesn't even enter our minds.

Soon everyone falls asleep, or so it seems. But I don't. I want to stay purposely awake to call back the day without anybody intruding on the silence. I want to think about the miracle, the unexpected luck that has come to me. I used to experience a burst of gladness in response to good luck and I keep expecting that feeling as I lie in the dark. But feeling eludes me. I try to force out the missing element that is needed to feel happiness. I try in vain. A blankness, which is a wall between me and my feelings, leaves me in despair. I want to call back something that has always been a part of me, but I find that its spot is empty. I have lost a part of myself. I want to cry but the tears won't come. An essential source, an affirmation of life, is gone. Finally I have to resign myself. I let my eyes wander through the dim naked hall and then to the group of sleeping girls close to me, and fall asleep without being able to grasp what freedom means to me.

Exuberant French singing wakes us the next morning. Stunned, we sit up and look at the stage, where the sound is coming from. We become even more puzzled at seeing a group of men who look like ex-prisoners, singing away while dancing on one leg, trying to put their trousers on. None of us heard them arrive during the night. It seems they stopped here by chance on their way to somewhere. Maybe home. Then they disappear as quickly as they arrived, leaving behind a spirit of cheerful revelry. It is as quick as a glance at a picture, but their energetic singing and uninhibited movements awake and liberate a hidden connection in us. They give us a small jolt toward life, a reminder that a real world exists beyond the boundaries of Germany.

We start to stir with more heart, thinking for the first time about what comes next. Then, by instinct rather than planning, we agree to look immediately for more permanent lodging. Since we sleep in our clothes and we know how to live without washing, there is nothing else to hold us back. We leave the hall promptly, each of us going her separate way to sample freedom independently, without even a friend's influence.

I wander between the houses, not knowing who I am, or what I am looking for, or what on earth I am doing here. I stray into a cottage occupied by a group of girls. I walk around by myself inside, in a no-man's land. No one gives me so much as a glance as I admire the beds, the dainty bedspread, the dressing table, the curtains, the mirror. I am face to face with myself, but I refuse to believe that the face gazing back from the mirror is mine. The last time I saw myself, my cropped head, was in a piece of broken glass in Auschwitz. The bedroom reflects back memories that rise slowly to the surface; memories of a warm home, a respectful household. Ironically, I reflect that just a day ago those rooms were someone's home, before the upheaval created by these tattered girls. I can relate clearly to the owner's state of mind in leaving it behind.

The girls are good-hearted and nice to me; they let me lie down for a nap, though their lodging is already filled. Only a crib is available. I climb in and fall asleep as soon as I curl up on the heavenly soft mattress. I have hardly started my cosy sleep when I wake with the feeling that someone is observing me. Lifting my head for a groggy gaze, I find myself staring at the most wonderful set of white teeth I have ever seen. It takes me a while to recognize and take in the whole picture of the owner of the benevolent grin, a black GI, who looks amused at the big baby in the crib. My awkward explanation, without the necessary words, is also a grin.

Impressed by the first encounter in my life with a black person, I remain propped up on my elbow, stunned. This encounter couldn't have happened to me before, in Middle-Europe, in Hungary. And what is more striking is that it happened just like that, so naturally: he simply walked in. The strangeness touches me, the strange change in which I find myself a player and which I now witness has just begun. It becomes suddenly clear. The first brush of a new culture. What a difference if a European uniformed soldier had walked in. What airs he would have manifested. The Americans in Europe. I am immensely proud of them, also very frightened by their newness. I am not sure. I am looking for the old Europe from before the war, to find my previous place. I just want to pick up where I left it. I also know that here is a change that can't be unmade. Will I be able to understand their easy smile? Will they be able to understand heavy-handed Europe with their American eyes?

Later, I watch the girls concocting a meal from reserves found in the pantry. They let me have some too, so I prepare to wash up the dishes in return. They look at me as though I've gone crazy. They take the plates away from me, open the window and simply fling the plates out of the second floor. "This is our dishwashing," they tell me. "Didn't they rob ours?"

"Yes, they did," I reply, but secretly the revenge scares me. I am frightened by anarchy without social norms. I walk away without so much as a goodbye.

———

On our third day in town, the German inhabitants are still in hiding. Only those living further out have stayed in their dwellings. It is in one of these homes that we eventually seek accommodation. We decide to approach the farmer's wife for a room. Apparently, she doesn't dare to refuse, so all ten of us move in. No doubt, judging by family members' furtive looks, they are worried, not knowing what kind of fugitives they are bound to let in.

The narrow room they provide gets crowded with all of us inside. When we stretch out for the night we cover the whole surface of the floor. Even the door gets blocked, but we don't mind the scarcity of space. Closing our own door behind us makes us feel cheerful, as if something decent and civilized has come our way.

The next day, the early morning sunshine filters through our narrow window from the farmer's fields. The first day I stay around the farm, privileged by my new existence—the garden, the space, the freshly ploughed fields, the budded fruit trees, the red-crested white rooster in the yard. The blond, rosy-cheeked farmer's wife rushes about, her chin pushed downward, eluding my glance. I can't guess what her thoughts are as she struggles to look indifferent, ignoring my presence. Her small children are teasing each other, rolling in the grass, as if I were not there.

Everyone except me walks to town, arriving, as they later tell me, when food is being distributed. American army supplies are given out by soldiers not prepared yet for our sudden appearance. Included is a big, white, square, fluffy thing like a cake. The bread. The girls also bring back sugar, margarine and Nescafe. For boiling our water we have the pot I took from the *Gasthaus*. Cups appear from somewhere. The first supper in our new household is bread and margarine topped with sugar, and the Nescafe. It tastes like food, it is like a feast. It isn't even spoiled by knowing that the door that leads to the kitchen, and from there to the anteroom, has been locked for the night by the German family. Our window is the only way out.

Then we spread our rags out on the floor, preparing our spots for the night. I lie down as we all do, but I toss and turn for hours. Finally unable to remain on the floor any longer, I step carefully over the girls on the floor and head towards the window. In the pitch dark I climb out and go around to the back of the house, to the outdoor toilet. Then I climb back in quietly and lie down again.

Still I can't fall asleep. I sit up wondering what else I can do for the rest of the night, only to see two of the other girls sitting on the windowsill riding-fashion, each heading in a different direction, crossing the sill with different purpose. One is going out, the other is coming in. When the three of us notice each other we can't silence our giggles. Then everybody props themselves up for a sleepy look and suddenly the room becomes as busy as a beehive, everybody jumping out of their rags and heading towards the window, relieved because no one else could sleep. For the remainder of the night there is always someone on the move towards the window or through it. The exodus goes on till morning, amid witty remarks and laughter. Everybody joins in the unexpected party, only interrupted occasionally by an audible, "Keep quiet. I want to sleep." But the endless laughter goes on uncontrollably; we behave as though we are totally drunk.

As silly as it was, the night's laughter proves a useful bridge to relaxed interaction between us the next day. It also helps us to learn again how to enjoy easy camaraderie. It is the first remembrance of the old life. We also get wiser, learning that coffee is like a narcotic in our fragile condition. We don't know ourselves how weak we are.

———

Unnoticed, a routine creeps into our days of freedom. Responsibilities turn up right at the beginning. Our provisions have to be picked up daily from the supply centre at the public school in town. Each of us has a job to do in our communal household, and we all do it willingly. I run the household and am the cook, because I have no patience with sewing. And maybe because I have experience from before, which my friends respect. It also seems that the least misunderstanding is brought to me.

Our provisions are mostly bread, sugar, margarine, molasses, potatoes, milk and oatmeal, all in abundance. There are a few eggs but no meat. We drink milk and sour milk and more milk (lacking a fridge) and oatmeal in every shape and form. To everyone's admiration, I create the first oatmeal cookie. It is a treat we had never heard of in Hungary. Sometimes I walk in the forest for hours in search of mushrooms to give variety to our diet. So habitual does the mushroom search become that in the end, no matter where I go, I can't lift my eyes off the ground.

I divide the cooked food equally among us, just as I did in the camp, where we got a loaf of bread to be divided among seven, nine or eleven people. We are not that hungry now, but much time will have to go by before we can relax about portions. I count and divide anything that is distributed to us, even the box of straight pins we get one day. I start counting out pins like any other serious distribution, but while I separate portions of straight pins I realize how laughable my conscientious activity has become.

Clothes and fabrics come in from mysterious sources as our roommates scour the village daily. The things they grab are sometimes useless. An old pair of laced men's shoes, size 12, is of no use to us and lies thrown into one corner, until the idea comes to me that perhaps a farmer can use them. Sure enough, we get a rooster in exchange. It needs plenty of cooking, that tough old rooster, but the shoes were not perfect either.

For weeks the main preoccupation for all seven hundred and thirty women in the village is to get out of their rags and into decent clothing. Some people seem to have a knack for getting things, but it is hard to get information from them as to how they actually do it. If I ask, "Where did you get that?" I get very vague answers. The usual is, "Comme ci, comme ça," along with a smile. Or, "I organized it." The goods were appropriated, pinched, stolen. That much is clear to me.

Our roommates soon begin to resent the fact that Hanna and I don't "organize" anything for the household. Finally we can't postpone it any longer and we go out to look for goods. But we don't know how to go about it. After much hesitation and wandering around, we choose a cottage to approach. We ring the bell and a German sticks his head out the door, asking what we want. We inquire, smiling abashedly, whether he can help us out with some clothes. His answer is a stern We have nothing. He speaks to us as if he were chasing stray dogs away, and he slams the door in our faces. Ashamed and embarrassed, we are left there like beggars. We know it well, the right way to speak would have been his way: stern and demanding. We are not adapting ourselves well to our changed roles. We still remember normal, civilized dealings.

We walk away from the door, not looking at each other and not putting any explanations into words. Aimlessly we trudge along the road, afraid to try our luck somewhere else, but not admitting it aloud. We just walk on until one of us notices something white lying on the road. Getting close, we realize it is a muddy pair of longjohns.

"Let's take it," Hanna says.

"I hate to touch them," I say, and hide my hands.

"We can wash them," she replies, and takes some scrap paper from her pocket to lift them. We take them because we need to prove we have some "organizing" skills. Luckily no one takes any notice of us arriving home with the muddy longjohns.

———

Eszter and Hanna sew their own clothes, and mine too, mostly from used clothes. There are no stores, but even if there were we have no money to purchase. So we fabricate something from anything that comes our way. If it is noticeable that it was used, they wash it. Otherwise, they take it apart to see and guess what can be made of it; a blouse, a skirt, or panties or a bra. They make panties and bras out of whatever they come across, seldom the appropriate fabric. The panties are made from a rough, steel-blue material. I suffer real cuts from their sharp edges. I call them my steel pants but, having no others, venture to wear them again and again.

As soon as a pair of panties and a bra are finished, we wear them to sunbathe on the grass. We don't realize that our sense of what "decently covered" means is not restored yet. We have lost sight of what is appropriate, being so often undressed and naked in front of our captors. To us it seems that the world has changed its social norms. Without the bounds of pre-set social conformities, our inventiveness is marvellously fresh and free of burdens. Soon we notice the linen floral curtains in the village, which quickly disappear from the windows. They become summer skirts, sewed feverishly together. Two huge pockets sewed on, handy for depositing found treasures, become the latest fashion.

Spring turns into summer. Daily we grow physically stronger. We live only for the moment, without dwelling on the past, without thinking about the future. We are emerging back into life without thinking about its purpose, without ever looking at a calendar. Hardly any of us even takes notice of the day when war ends in Europe.

In the meantime, the Americans leave and the British take over Westfalen, the province we are in. The change makes no difference to us other than the fact that one day we are all invited for five o'clock tea to an English army camp. We don't know what to make of it, but go anyway in the army trucks that come to pick us up.

We arrive at a hall in the middle of a park. We unload. Inside, tables are set for tea, the army jazz band is playing. We all run inside blindly and grab a chair fast, as though our survival depends on it. Englishmen shyly approach us to dance. The conversation is mostly guesswork, since no one speaks anyone else's language. Later, tea, sandwiches and biscuits are served. All the food disappears in seconds. The big pockets on the summer skirts fill up with booty, and that includes hastily gathered cigarette butts, too. We don't even inspect the typically English triangles of paper-thin sandwiches for their contents. We eat them or bury them in our pockets for later.

The teas continue throughout the summer months and we continue going, to get out of our own circle. But mostly we go to fill up our pockets and for the food we get there.

———

The days pass unnoticed. I am unable to occupy my mind with anything other than trivial, momentary worries. My mind functions as if I were in an empty world. No ties. Unattached. No past. I don't dare to ask myself about it, or question my friends about their worries, though I sense that they are deliberately not discussing their concerns with me. They never put them into words. I guess my tragedy, but never let them know. I fool them with my silence. I laugh a lot of hysterical laughter while trembling inside.

The girls come back one day from town to say that they have heard about a transport back to Hungary. They find the connection and decide to go. I am going, too.

We travel with high hopes for a whole day and half a night on a rented truck, only to realize that we are entangled in a complicated political game between the Russians, Americans and British. We are stopped and taken to an English Army camp, where an old English colonel, awakened by our arrival in the middle of the night, hobbles in on his walking stick (the inheritance of a noble lineage) to make a great to-do over the important task of making tea for us. He no doubt feels uncomfortable with the lie he is supposed to tell us concerning why we can't go further. Every few seconds he examines his tea closely, turns it with a wooden spoon, sniffs it, and again covers it. It has to be perfect tea, fit for a noble Englishman. It is truly perfect, but that is scant consolation when our truck is turned back, with close to a hundred girls in it, to the village.

A few weeks later, Hanna and I decide to try the road again, but this time on our own. Eszter is wavering, can't make up her mind whether to go with us or stay. Her decision is made easier by the unexpected news, brought by visitors from Hungary, that her fiancé has married someone else. She stays.

It is August 1945 and very hot. We struggle through five days of travelling. We travel by trains run only randomly, and overloaded down to their stairs. Sometimes we sit in open box-cars without roofs, fully exposed to the sun, all in a sweat, bespeckled with flakes of soot that stick to us. We proceed by foot on stretches where the railway line is in ruins, to wait at bombed-out or half-bombed stations for a train which will eventually arrive. We even risk hitchhiking on trucks that take us along even further on the road to our goal, which is Passau, the city at the German-Austrian border.

When I think of the city Passau, the Danube inevitably comes into my mind. I see it vividly as it rolls on and on along the landscape, becoming more generous toward Budapest. I feel it is so close I could touch it as it rolls through the city. Longingly, I follow the familiar map, which I perceive as my own past, as it changes course there and turns downward, running along the Balkans, following more rugged landscapes and facing more exotic people as it rushes towards the Black Sea.

At last we stand on its shores. I look at its ripples. The water is not blue. It is brown and filthy. Dirty remains of war are floating on it. We inquire. Masses of people have been living for months near the river in damaged railway cars, waiting to cross the border into Austria. Panic comes over me.

"Hanna, I can't go any further."

"Why, what has happened?" she asks.

"I can't go back to Hungary. I can't go back." I don't know why I am scared. I can't think through why this is so. My illusion and longing have turned into fright.

Without any further word or question, my friend makes the five-day trip back to Westfalen with me again. But Hungary remains her ultimate goal.

A few weeks later, Hanna leaves. It is already close to nightfall when I accompany her into town to meet her party. On the way we decide to say only a brief farewell to spare ourselves painful emotions. I know I will go home to an empty room, because Eszter has moved in with another friend. After a determinedly courageous handshake we turn our backs on each other and depart in different directions. Unhurried, I take the winding farm roads back to our room. Loud emptiness greets me as I open the door. Now it is mine alone. I don't turn the light on. It would be too harsh. I open the window and sit in semi-darkness. Only the sound of creatures settling before they sleep for the night comes in from outside. I sit empty, without thoughts. I have nothing to think about. I don't know how to start my life again.

What Remains

The Recipe Book

It might have started on a specially hungry day, this recalling of recipes.

"Chocolate, eggs, the nuts and the butter." "Stir it till fluffy. . . ." ". . . fold it carefully. . . ."

Around us everything was grey. The factory, the machines, the sky, the women, their faces, their tattered rags; all was grey, hopelessly grey, and we were starving.

". . . for holidays I used to make it, this chocolate-cream-filled torte, I decorated it with candied nuts. . . ."

I listened, ashamed of the fool in me who even felt like listening to circumstances which had never existed or, if they had, no longer counted. I was ashamed to let myself be drawn in, as if unaware of present reality. As if unaware of the question, "What's the use?"

But a strong distant picture demanded voice: the loving labour of preparing it, and the devotion, art and beauty in its creation, the pride, the respect on those faces around the festive table who knew a TORTE's deeper meaning.

I jotted down all that I could.

I jotted it down on scrap paper found in trash cans in the factory—taken, stolen. They were pieces covered in pencilled recordings of German workers' wages, but I overlooked the words underneath. I wrote the ingredients down, hardly able to grip the stump of a pencil, the recipes of nameless women—whoever happened to pass by. I kept writing down the ingredients, words enshrouded in secret meaning and language in my mind. They were accompanied by a distant sound—the promising, bell-like music of my mother's copper bowl as she beat egg whites by hand, coming through the open kitchen door to find me standing in the backyard in the Easter sunshine.

I kept recording recipes, whatever anyone could remember.

Unnoticed was the delicate idea of my friend Eszter, who collected my scraps of paper and bound them into a recipe book which she returned to me as a gift.

The motivation to do it and the effort to create it was more than this mere picture can show.

It was done at a time when we had only our bare body and nothing more. When a handkerchief or a piece of paper for washroom use was thought of as too humane for us. We lived without.

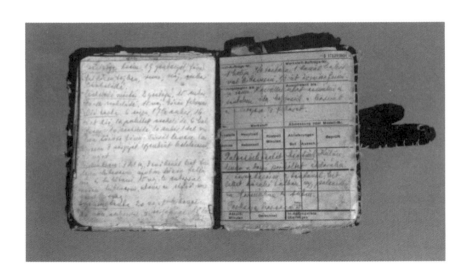

She made the cover from oil-soaked rags she had spotted in garbage cans. She washed them in cold water, without soap. She used black ones for the cover and pulled pieces of thread from lighter ones to embroider it. She took scrap metal, the ends of hand grenades, and a small file to make the decoration: THE POT. All were smuggled out under the risk of her being beaten severely if discovered. To bring the unfinished work together she had to find a woman among the six hundred who had a needle, someone who was willing to trust a needle to a woman she didn't know, and had also the heart to put up with the inconvenience. She carried it out after her twelve-hour work shift.

Though the product was a demonstration of her respect for my endeavour, Eszter couldn't have guessed how far this little book would take me later. I have cherished the recipe book for over fifty-three years. It served as my only link with freedom and normalcy, even long after the war.

Sadly, I lost touch with Eszter in 1946 in the chaos of postwar Europe.

Walnut Torte

6 yolks, 17-1/2 sugar, 14 ground walnuts, 10 chocolate softened, 6 beaten egg whites.
Cream: 10 chocolate, 10 sugar, 1 dcl water, all mixed and warmed. Add 3 yolks, one by one, when cooled to lukewarm, then beat in 15 butter.

Chestnut-cream

1 kg chestnuts, cooked in milk. Add rum, butter, sugar, chocolate to taste.

(Hungarian recipes don't direct every movement because the culture assumes cooks know. The measurements are in the metric system.)

Häftling 168 (Convict 168)

Häftling 168 was my number, that was all the SS needed to know about me. It was hung on my neck (with different string) in Auschwitz before I was shipped to the factory, and was to be worn all the time.

Mezuzah

The small case, called Mezuzah in Hebrew, means doorpost. Inside are quotations from the Bible rolled in parchment. It is usually put on doorposts, but it can also be worn.

The aperture on it reveals the word "Almighty."

The Mezuzah was given to us, along with a prayer book, a few days after our liberation, by an American chaplain who happened to pass by.

The Child's Head

The child's head with the bonnet was chiseled by Hannah. She gave it to me and I wore it on a string as a necklace. I wore it only to honour her work, but with great reluctance. I didn't want to believe that Hannah was suggesting that something tragic had happened.

Hannah was a talented creator. She could give character to her objects with a few decisive strokes, whether with metal or by drawing. Some sought her out to place an order for a locket or a medallion, mainly as an icon or an illusion for something to love amid the cold existence.

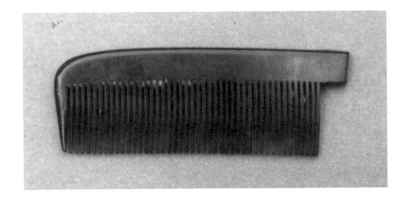

The Comb

The broken comb was one item I claimed proprietary rights to as I bought it for two slices of bread out of my daily ration. Hannah or Eszter helped me to negotiate the deal. Not that I needed a comb badly when my hair started to grow, but I knew where there is hair there is supposed to be a comb. As it turned out later, it saved me from having head lice.

These kinds of exchanges for food were common, and we soon found a general name for the items. We called them "Starvedforyou."

The Picture Book

The sewed-together felt pages, the picture book, is a keepsake from Eszter. It looks as if it were a hat in its previous life. Its contents are a demonstration of the creative urge to make objects that could not be found within prison walls. The snowdrop, sailing board, cloverleaf. Remarkable is the red shred of cloth stitched on the cover like a bow.

Elisabeth Raab, 1953, Quito, Ecuador

Elisabeth

Henry

David

Robert

1962. Leaving Quito, Ecuador

Elisabeth Raab, 1988, Budapest, Hungary, the Danube
in the background

The Return

Months later, Hanna manages to get a letter to me. It begins, "Dear lonely bird." She writes that she and her husband found each other, that they settled in the family business house, that they have a circle of young friends to get together and socialize with, and that she has clothes and things that we could only dream of in camp. She says she expects her first baby in July 1946. She also tells me that my husband has returned home, too, and is expecting me back.

Her letter, with its vision of a home, makes me tremble, causing me to doubt my present, my chosen solitude. But at the same time, as if in a paralyzing trance, I can't see myself in any circle or in any environment. I don't feel I belong anywhere. I have no aspirations left. I wait for I don't know what. I wait for time to tell me. I am unable to build anew on the ruins of my life.

I am not capable of recognizing, in 1945, what it is I am doing. Is it weakness or strength or shock that holds me inescapably?

———

At the beginning of the winter, Eszter realizes that she feels closer to me than to her other friend. She moves back to stay, but it is not the same any more with our trio reduced to two. We are simply two lonely birds rather than one. Eszter is six years my junior and respects my experience and judgment, which makes it doubly hard for me because I am not sure I am still good at anything. Our only positive contribution to each other is that we are not alone.

There is not much in the village to keep us busy, especially in the winter months. We do not even have books to read. One of our chores is to pick up our daily food supply and, once a month, a parcel that is sent from America by a Jewish charity organization, the Joint Distribution Committee, JOINT. This usually contains some delicacies like sardines, salami, canned salmon, cigarettes and cigars. We make some money on the cigars, selling them to local farmers. Used American clothes are also taken in and distributed by those of our people who run the depot. Eszter alters the clothes to our measurements. I help her, or knit if I can get wool. Usually Eszter is the one who picks up the charity goods. She likes these excursions to the village, and brings home "sensational" gossip, like who is doing what and who is squabbling with whom and what people predict in general. She does that much better than I would. She is good at socializing, whether in the food line or on the street corners.

From time to time, we take the train to one of the two closest cities, Gütersloh or Bielefeld, for no particular reason except that the fare is only pennies. On one of our trips, German teenagers shout at us in the train, "Go back to Palestine." I am not surprised at their contaminated ideology. I expect them to dislike us. The family we live with never addresses a word to us or asks anything. It is as if we were transparent. Only their maid, an old woman, acknowledges us, rapping on our window secretly at night to hand in some leftovers, when she has them.

One morning in January, I must pick up the milk because Eszter is sick with a cold. As I don't think my light shoes from the JOINT parcel will do in the thick frozen snow, I pull my old wooden camp clogs out from under the bed and put them on. As

I am waiting for my turn in the milk line the man from the clothing depot approaches me.

"Do you realize that it is January 1946 now, and you are still wearing your wooden clogs?" he says. "I'll give you a pair of shoes."

A little embarrassed, like one who is caught doing the wrong thing, I say, "That is really thoughtful of you." I anticipate something extraordinary.

To my dismay, he comes back carrying a pair of black-laced men's shoes, and oversized too. However, I have trouble refusing them. I have difficulty shaming and exposing him, though I know he has better ones inside. Whoever handles the depot has favourite people for whom they keep the best items. I could accept and understand that at the camp, where every morsel was a question of life and death, but it bothers me now. Some are unable to leave the camp morals behind them. Some continue to tell lies and draw advantages from the power of the smallest office. Communal life is certainly not for me. I am not good at confrontations, and communal life is full of them.

———

Although neither the mails nor the railways are functioning regularly, by some mysterious means I receive a letter. My brother Miki's writing is on the envelope. I open it, dizzy with excitement, and take the pictures out of it. One is of Miki himself. The other is my father's last portrait. I read the accompanying letter from Miki with rising hope, but reading it further I find that my hidden fear is reality. Finally, it is confirmed that my father, like my mother and daughter, did not return from camp. I don't dare to realize what that means. Furthermore, Miki wonders why I haven't come back to Hungary. How come everybody who has been liberated is back, except me? I have no reply to his question.

Winter turns into spring and I speak with Eszter more often about a trip to Hungary. Maybe in the summer, we say. About this time I meet a man, a D.P. (displaced person) like me. Nathan, also recently liberated, is from Poland. He has come to town to find his sister and her husband. We become friends and we seem to understand each other well and to share a general view of life, in spite of our fifteen-year age difference. Within weeks of our meeting, more relatives of his turn up, including one of his brothers. Then more friends arrive, and acquaintances of his from back home. Everybody is welcome. They come and go, sleep where there is room, eat and drink what they can find. It is a busy, warm, open household, and our connection with it does a world of good to Eszter's and my life.

———

At the beginning of June, my trip with Eszter takes shape. My new friend Nathan doesn't want me to go, but at the same time he is aware that I have to accomplish what I have taken upon myself. He even contributes fifty dollars towards my trip, which is a lot of money and great help. We add it to the meagre cigar money we have put aside.

We start out, as planned, in June 1946 by train, heading east. From one D.P. camp to the next, we go step by step, finding accommodations where we can sleep, shower and have a bowl of soup. At every camp, we get new information from other travellers about which camp should be our next stop and how to get there. The last and longest stay is at Pocking, where we stagnate on the German side of the Austrian border. Pocking is an exodus junction from the East to the West and from the West to the East. People are searching for ideals, ideologies, a home, security, relatives. The names they give to their goals are different, but the meaning is the same: a place to settle.

From the East, uprooted people see their destination in some faraway place, where life and happiness and everything else will fall into place if they simply land there. Each one's hope is fixed on a faraway land, a sparkling point on the horizon one hasn't quite discovered yet. Neither its language, its people, its history, its geography, or its climate is known. One only knows that it is a country far away, a refuge where life will begin again. To leave Europe behind means a whole new start. For many of us it is the only dream we have left to hold on to.

The majority of travellers come from Siberia, where many Polish Jews hid during the war. After the war, with great effort, they made their way back to Poland, only to find they are not welcomed. It is a dangerous place for Jews to live, even after the war.

The family that sleeps on the straw sack closest to me, consisting of parents, children and grandparents, is typical. At the onset of war they left Poland and wandered a thousand miles to safety in Siberia, waiting for the war's end. When at last it came, after six years, they started to move on toward Poland, hoping to live there as before. But when it turned out that the Poles' hatred went as far as murder, they rushed from place to place, heading toward the West through Hungary, Austria and ironically, to Germany. There somehow they got in touch, after a long tedious wait, with a relative who lived in Brazil. They have never even seen the relative. Now, when I meet them, they hope every day for the arrival of a visa from Brazil, which has been promised to them for months. The children are touching. I hear the little boy, aged seven, asking about Brazil. He hears the name so often, especially in connection with anything they have a desire to do. The answer is always the same. "Not now, but in Brazil." He doesn't know what that means, or what a permanent home means.

I hear him asking his mother, "And where do we go from Brazil?"

A restless wanderlust sweeps through Europe, a result of the war. Being without social responsibility, without roots, often doesn't bring out the best in people. A nasty experience at

Pocking teaches me about danger. I am sitting on my straw sack, with my back to the door, when a man grabs me from behind and holds me down with crazy kisses. No one is around to help. To get rid of him I bite hard on his lip and he loosens his grip. Disgusted when I see the blood spurting from his lip, I hold back my tears, feeling angry and debased by his attack and because of the cruelty I was forced into.

We spend four weeks in Pocking, in depressing conditions, before we dare to move on. By accident, Eszter meets Steve there; he is a Hungarian from Pécs whom she knew before the war. Then we run into a woman from our camp, Paula. So we become a group with the same goal, to go back to Hungary.

Eszter's friend Steve thinks the best route is to go to Salzburg first, which is the closest city to Pocking, and, from there, through Vienna to Budapest. He wants to try it by himself first, he says, and then come back for the rest of us.

"I want to try it with you," I say. Being at the limit of my patience in Pocking, I will try anything. "I have a cousin somewhere in Salzburg where I could wait for all of you," I argue. "Then we can continue together from there."

So that is what we do.

I pack my few possessions into my knapsack, fill my canteen with water and am ready for the trip. In the pitch-dark we approach the station and hide in its darkest corner at the far end of the platform, flattening ourselves behind the wall. From there we can watch the freight train when it comes in. The single small bulb over the station's door suits us just fine. We hope to remain unnoticed.

In silent suspense we wait for the moment to arrive. At 11:00 p.m. we spot the bright goggle eyes of the train advancing through the darkness. The noise is ear-splitting. Knapsacks in hand, we stay hidden until it stops. Then we approach, throw our knapsacks with a strong toss onto the top of the second-last car, which has stopped in front of our hiding spot. Swiftly, we climb up after them. It is an open freight car filled to the top with coal. We dig in fast and cover ourselves up with coal. We hear voices and boots coming very close and fear we have been noticed. We have no idea what will happen if we are caught. Probably jail. We hardly dare to breathe. Minutes later, a whistle, a jerky pull, and we are moving away from Pocking.

Irreversibly now, we are pulled into the hollow of night. Hour after hour, our monotonous advance continues. From time to time we lift our heads to look into the hazy, warm August night, passing woods and cornfields, signs of settled people's lives. After a couple of hours I forget anything else, preoccupied with the sharp edge of every piece of coal digging into me with every bump the train makes. For weeks my body will bear the black and blue souvenirs of that trip.

Around 6:00 a.m., the train begins to slow down. It drags into a station and comes to a screeching stop. We lift our heads slightly. The dark silhouettes of mountains appear on the horizon. The Alps at Salzburg. It is just about daybreak. The contours are still veiled in a light haze. The city is breathing quietly. The air smells humid and warm, like before a very hot summer day, but still with the lingering freshness of the night. I wish I could take part in it with a free heart. My longing is vivid, the atmosphere awakes feelings from my past. I envy the Salzburgers, who are still stretched out between their white linen sheets, anticipating a beautiful summer day when they rise to a fresh coffee and a new day. I also envy their unmarked consciences, continuing their lives the way they are used to.

We hear the boots of the American border guards and their conversation. The sound of their boots is getting closer. They stop at the last car. We don't know what to do or what to think. We wait. Then their footsteps fade. We start to pick up our knapsacks when we hear them coming in our direction again. We lie down as fast as we can, in the same spot in the coal. We hear them climbing onto every car. I sense a light. I hold my breath. I begin to resign myself to being caught, feel the flashlight sliding over me. But by some miracle they climb down again, and I understand one word of what they say in English while walking away. "Mistake." I breathe it to Steve: "Mistake."

Without waiting an extra moment, we throw our knapsacks down between the trains and, simultaneously, we jump down. We hear the Americans shouting and running, but we crawl under the next train and then run as fast as we can, over rails, under wagons, to cross the enormous railway junction, until we find a gap in the far fence. We run into a back alley toward a bombed-out house, into its garden, running between the overgrown weeds, to an old car without wheels. I push its hanging door aside, clear the spider webs from the opening and drop panting on its dust covered beige leather seat. For long minutes we don't utter a word.

Later, we wash our coal-blackened faces and hands from the canteen I carry. We want to look decent, not suspiciously illegal on the streets of Salzburg.

At 8:00 a.m., the sun is already hot and we are out walking and deliberating how to find my cousin. I have heard he is working for a relief organization, set up after the war. We ask, and are sent from one place to another and one office to the next, until we are ready to give it up. Then someone gives us a new lead, and we continue to search the unfamiliar city with fresh hope.

At noon, we find ourselves ringing the bell of my cousin's apartment. His new wife opens the door. She is easy to speak to, kind and friendly, and takes us in at once. I haven't seen my cousin for years, and he is not enthusiastic about seeing me now. He greets me with indifference, and with what is to me a striking coolness. I try to explain it away by his terrible wartime experience. I know he went through much more than I did. Grudgingly, he lets me stay with them—for only a few days, he says, because his landlord, like many Austrians, is eager to denounce anybody illegal to the authorities.

Steven returns the next day for Eszter and Paula. I plan to meet them in about four days. I don't move around the city much for fear of being caught, but try at least to be useful at home. I help to prepare meals and, the second day of my stay, I make the dessert. We sit at the table without a word. My cousin eats his meal with a stern face, looking into his plate. It is when he has the second spoonful of my dessert in his mouth that his facial expression softens. He lifts his eyes from his plate and glances at me, then in slow motion his face transforms itself almost into a smile. I know the taste reminds him of something. My mother and his mother were sisters.

Over the next few days I concentrate my thoughts mostly on how I will get through all the zones, Austrian, American, British, Russian, which lie ahead between Salzburg and Hungary. My movement is limited, but I make anxious inquiries to the few people I meet, without any results. It already looks hopeless, when by chance a man who can make legitimate-looking papers comes to visit my cousin. I will be able to cross borders with these false papers. In exchange, he wants me to smuggle cigarettes to his parents in Hungary. Cigarettes are a coveted means of exchange, a substantial help to his parents. I take the offer. I am clear about the danger, but then again, my entire trip is nothing but danger.

In the meantime, the expected four days go by. Then a whole week passes without a word from Eszter, Steven and Paula. I wait another two days, and then I have to move on. I don't want to use up my cousin's hospitality, nor do I feel comfortable with his Austrian neighbours. Without knowing Eszter's whereabouts I go, hoping to meet her at Hanna's in Pécs.

I board the Alberg-Express to Budapest via Vienna. My luggage consists of a knapsack and a corrugated paper box. Uneasily, I look for a good place for it, and a seat for myself. There are no seats left, I realize, concerned, but maybe that's better with my hot paper box. Timidly, I put the cigarette-filled parcel down, away from me in case it is discovered, so it won't

101

look like mine. At the same time I stand close enough to keep an eye on it, if someone tries to take it. Several times I have to push it unnoticed in front of me with my foot between people's feet in the crowded passageway. It is mine and it is not mine. Because I am totally illegal, my heart beats fast as I pass, with much luck, through all four pass-controls and each luggage-control.

En route to Budapest, the train passes through Győr, the city once closest to me. As it is a major station, the train stays for a while. I step to the window and, with fake fortitude, pull it down to face the city. The humid summer air rushes at once into my face. I savour the dizzying, deep breath of it. It is eerie that it is the same. It hasn't changed since I emerged daily from this station on those hot days, running impatiently, sweating all the more, to cool off in the Danube. Nervously, my eyes comb the platform and the station's building. It is just as before. It is as if time stood still, as if nothing has happened. I was not here, but life went on as if I were. It is as if, since then, the station attendants have been standing in the same uniforms, holding the same signals, Stop or Go, with the same whistle between their lips, blowing the same tune. It is only I who am not the same. I listen to my memories from the time I was at this station twice a day and was intimate with it, when I knew this city in its every corner, in its every mood, in its every season. Then it was my middle-class nest. But now is now. All that doesn't count anymore. Empty and void, I don't ask questions. I don't want to judge. And still, with timid feelers, I want to hold onto a past that I can't bring myself to abandon.

On the way to Budapest, when I remind myself that I am in the middle of a real world and I have to look acceptable and civilized as if nothing has happened, I open my heart to the innocent August scenery. I am conscious of being in Hungary, the place I have held for so long in my secret thoughts, and so far away. The stubble fields, the cornfields, the sugar beets, the acacia trees. Now I don't know what to feel—without hate, and without the love I try to repress.

It is quite hot in the late afternoon on August 8 when I come out from the West railway station in the heart of Budapest. People rush by and mind their own business. They don't find me strange with my knapsack, my cheap, makeshift summer dress, my ill-fitting shoes without socks. It is as if they believe I have been here all these years, as they have. On these dusty, unkempt grey streets, they walk, some in neat, some in worn-out clothes, looking down at their feet with straining necks, as if pulling a heavy load. All have drab faces, slumped shoulders, the men and women all carrying something. No one glances at me, or takes me for an alien. Only I feel strange in this environment. I used to come here first class, by sleeping car, for one-day business trips, looking forward to a busy day after a well-rested night. A hundred years ago.

I search in my bag for my brother's address and start to speculate on how to get there. After two hours of errors and mistakes, worn out, I finally find the street and the number. It is a rental building with a wide entrance gate under the second-floor apartment. The entrance is as long as the apartment is wide, Budapest-fashion. The long entrance takes me into a square, paved courtyard. I find Miki sitting on the back porch fence, in conversation with people. When he notices me he jumps off at once and rushes to greet me. Many times I have imagined the moment I'll meet him again. The pillars of a whole world—our world—have collapsed since we last saw each other. We hug, but we don't cry. We say nothing sentimental. We are too shy. He looks great; he is twenty-one.

He introduces me to the family on the first floor, where he takes his meals, and he says that I can stay there, too. His relationship with the family is not clear to me, until he tells me that he has opened a car repair shop with the son. But Miki himself has a sublet room on another floor in the same building. I accept Miki's suggestion to stay with the family, as I have

103

no other place to stay. I also think that I will only stay for short intervals, since I have various trips in mind.

During the first two days of my stay with Miki we catch up on a few matters, as I tell him about Germany and my eventual return there. He tells me about the situation with him, and in Hungary generally. We speak mostly about business; he tells me very little about his private life or his relationships with people. I feel he is disappointed in me, that he expected more of my business talent to come out. But I am simply not capable. My loss is more than the naked eye can see. He doesn't interpret my silence for what it is. He believes strongly it is bad will on my part, and I am not good at explaining, especially when it means defending myself. To my great regret, it becomes apparent that we are no support to each other, that we see the world differently, though we started out with mutual roots. We start to deal with each other only on the surface, and this becomes more than just unsettling to me in my already unsettled state. His girlfriend, who was the perfect person for him, regrettably didn't return from the concentration camp.

I make Pécs my first choice, to go and see Hanna. Maybe Eszter has arrived in the meantime. Before I leave, I telephone the people whose cigarettes I have brought, and tell them to pick them up any time while I am away. I purchase a ticket for the evening train with the thought that night travelling won't be as crowded. Disappointed, I stand the whole night through.

Over-filled trains, restless travelling, this postwar phenomenon has caught on even in Hungary. Everyone is going somewhere else: some to piece life together again, others to find themselves. Like the poet who, in the dark, after a few intense scrutinizing glares, moves unpleasantly close to recite his poems to me. The circumstances are most unpoetic, the environment unattractive in the dark, dirty train. He recites his poems at the broken window, but he is driven like a lonely soul with the need to throw out his feelings to a sympathetic listener.

The mutilated trains are painful to look at. They are an accusing finger pointed at humans' boundless craziness. On this one, the blown-out windows with not a single pane left are like dark, fixed eyes. The draft blows through them the whole night. The damage is too deep ever to be righted. Yet the trains still continue their tasks, dutifully carrying the remnants of war, while the past is engraved on them. They tell about the bombing, the shooting, the escapees, the troop transports, the running away, the deportations, the deserters, the Jews, the occupations, the wounded, the homeless, the hounded, the hatred, and the loneliness that is greater than words will ever be able to express.

When I leave, descending the train's stairs into the early morning sunshine, I feel its pain transferred, like a friend's, into me.

I am back in Pécs once more. It has been close to two-and-a-half years since I left. It seems like centuries. Clandestinely, I leave the railway station step by step, putting my feet down on the sidewalk, aware of every improbable sensation on Zsolnay Street. I chase away all coherent memories and thoughts in the fear I'll go insane, till I arrive at Deák Street, where Hanna lives. It is early, but having a baby just a few weeks old she must certainly be up. I stop at the house and whistle our old signal under the window, "Regen Tropfe." Promptly the window is flung open on the second floor. Hanna glances down.

"Böske!" she shouts. "One second. I'll throw the key down." It is simple. Just like that.

She runs down the stairs to meet me halfway. We hug and walk up the stairs, arms on each other's shoulders, as if we had parted only yesterday. No introduction. No explanation.

I am also welcomed by her husband, just like before the war. He always willingly accepted her friends. Then she shows me her home and introduces me to her four-week-old daughter. "This is Eva Katalin," she says.

The baby's name stabs my heart. She has given her the name Katalin in memory of my daughter. I should acknowledge it and take her gesture as lovingly generous. But I have no words. I can only smile, slightly. She is not hurt. I am sure she understands me.

I offer to sleep in the same room with the baby to relieve Hanna for the short time of my stay. She looks unusually worn out, which is no wonder; she is having problems with an infected breast. I accompany her daily to the hospital, to the maternity ward, to change the dressing and draining tube. We walk daily along roads so familiar to me. I keep my memories to myself. There is no need to exchange thoughts. I know she can read them without words. I feel free with them, Hanna and her husband, and comfortably fall into step with their everyday routine. I consider their accomplishment a major miracle, along with those of the few friends I meet who are all adjusting to normalcy so soon.

For me, it is too short a time after our cataclysm and the irreplaceable losses to pick up the threads and continue in an organized middle-class life. For me, the peril is not that far behind me yet. I feel as much an outsider here as in Germany. I am not able to identify with any society, much as I long for peace. But I am most happy for Hanna. It is wonderful that her life looks so beautifully reassuring. Her husband has picked up his furniture manufacturing business from before. They get together with old friends, also with new ones. Hanna is a very gracious hostess, so people appreciate being her guest.

The unpleasant task of meeting my husband is still ahead. It worries me. But Hanna is there to give a hand and invites him to meet me under her protection as a hostess. He was always easily enraged, and I find myself wondering now, with apprehension, what this encounter will bring.

He arrives with a friend of his. Hanna lets them in and then I go to greet them. When I approach Imre, an awkward situation arises; somehow, I get too close for a handshake. We realize it, and stop. In the end, our greeting results in a curiously angled handshake. Hanna motions us to sit down. Meanwhile, we manage to overcome the painful mistake when we start to chat. He sits opposite me. I find him older than when I saw him last. His hair, as he always feared, is thinner. Looking at him, I feel shy and outlandish in my outfit, embarrassed, like an impoverished relative demoted from her previous position. I am aware that I am not the way he must have kept me in his mind.

However, our civilized conversation goes better than I thought it would, though the air is loaded with unspoken thoughts. I am sure that the mediating presence of his and my friends helps us avoid terribly hurtful words. Sitting across from him, I manage to settle down and neutralize my feelings and rest my eyes on him calmly. I can even recognize his effort to look impeccable, just like before, though I see a carefully mended buttonhole on his lapel. That makes me think that it is a second-hand suit, worked over by a skilful tailor.

When they leave, we have agreed to a meeting, just the two of us, the next day. Imre comes to meet me at the plaza where our business was before. He has opened it again, and wants me to go and see the shop. Uncomfortably, I do. I meet the previous employees that he has taken back. I greet them as if I were a casual acquaintance and keep myself disengaged. Then on the way out, crossing the plaza, I see the mailman's lean, tall figure coming closer from the opposite direction. Easy to recognize, he looks the way he always did, a symbol of the proud Hungarian civil service of bygone times. Dressed precisely, respectfully, in the correct manner, just as I remember him. Even his moustache is twirled like before. He approaches with the same old bearing, the same old gait, just as he did when he handed me the daily mail in the mornings at my desk in the store, when I would ask, "Anything for me?" hoping to find among the business letters a letter from home.

He used to say, "Today I bring some good mail to you, Madame." And now I hear him saying in his warm-hearted, jovial voice, "I am so glad to see you back, Madame."

Fragments and pictures: the shop, the mailman, my husband create a momentary and deceptive illusion that the past is in the present. In a sudden panic I think: What if I stay?! Am I doing the right thing to reject all this?

But the answer soon follows. I see clearly that the differences between us are insurmountable. Though Imre suggests this morning that I should stay, I remember his uncontrollable anger, his wrath, and his jealousy bordering on insanity. I know that the road back is closed for me. I have to remain steadfast, in spite of the pain that is not yet ended.

Alone

After I have spent eight days in Pécs, Eszter still hasn't shown up. We worry and we don't know what to think, but restlessness overcomes me. I won't wait. Instead, I promise Hanna to come back again. By then, I am sure, I'll find Eszter there, too. I take the rickety train again, travelling at night to arrive in Budapest totally worn out. I go to see Miki and stay with the same family as before. In reality, my stop-gap stay with them doesn't make the days pleasant. Rather, I feel as though I am on the way somewhere else all the time. I also find that some money I had hidden in my knapsack was taken in my absence, but I am ashamed to ask about it.

While I exchange information with Miki, I learn happily about a few returned cousins: Ivan, who has settled temporarily in Szemere, and Ditta, who is staying for the moment with her mother's cousin not far from here. And two aunts are in Czechoslovakia. I realize that my dearest uncle, my late grandfather's younger brother, is alive and is in Budapest. He is now in his late seventies and still practising dentistry. How often I had him in mind in camp, hoping and doubting. I am overjoyed. I make plans with Miki to go to Győr and Szemere together, but, before anything, I want to see Uncle Mano.

Memorable moments from my childhood burst like happy balloons on my way to his apartment. The memories I retained from the times when he used to visit us in Szemere for a week or longer a few times every year. He never let us know he was coming; he was just suddenly at the door, opening it softly, looking through the door with a kind, mischievous, silent smile. I recall particularly that special morning when my mother stood me up on a chair to dress me. At the very moment she was pulling off my pyjamas I spotted a cautious gap widening at the door. I jumped off, uncontrollably, undressed as I was, and ran to him to hang on his neck, calling "Uncle Mano, Uncle Mano," never wanting to let him go. He coaxed me back somehow to stand on the chair again while he produced a necklace to hang on my neck right away, though I was still naked. I could hardly be calmed down long enough to be dressed.

He was a master of producing such surprises, but even if he had come without one I would have loved him just the same. The days were special for me while he visited. It was the same for my brother Miki, or my two cousins, his grand-nephew and niece, Ditta and Ede. We loved his appreciation of us, his joyous acknowledgment of every little foolish thing we said or did. He found it all fabulous. He was a true children's friend, an avant garde in children's psychology when others still accepted the saying that was the rule among adults: children should be seen but not heard.

No wonder I hung on to every minute of the day. Except after lunch, when I felt deprived as he returned to his room for his siesta. Then I tiptoed constantly under his window, hoping to find the folding shutters open.

One small incident comes back to me: the moment when I noticed how unusually short he was. I was about five and had probably grown since his last visit. After our ritual of emotional greeting I said, stepping back a bit: "Uncle Mano, you are so small."

My father didn't know what to say; nothing could have been appropriate. "You hurt your uncle," he said.

The fact that I had hurt him didn't leave my mind for weeks, until the next chance came to ease my own hurt. It happened that a few weeks later he made a stopover on his way back from his vacation. As soon as I caught sight of him, I clapped my hands happily, feigning surprise, and exclaimed: "Oh, Uncle Mano, you grew!"

I find him now at the same address, in the same condominium he lived in before. It is a magical address in my memory: 21. Terez Ring. For others, just a number and a street. For me, this intimate, special-sounding place hid a personal friend of mine and a benevolent friend of every living soul, one who refused to notice anything but beauty. He receives me unaltered, in his usual quiet manner. It is so good to see him. Someone from my childhood and so close to my heart. I have a lump in my throat at first. Probably he does, too. The conversation starts slowly, as we find ourselves searching for words. My adoration for him was childlike, and now, a grownup, alone, who has been through so much, I am scared to let myself speak about it. And he doesn't want to speak about his sad times either. We don't dare to ask each other. We face each other somewhat embarrassed, holding back so much untouchable pain that it paralyzes our tongues. We hide behind face-saving masks, ashamed of our deluded trust in humanity.

At last he finds something to say: "Come, I'll show you a miracle." He takes me into his office and points to the bullet holes in the wall. "Here's why these devils couldn't take my dentist's chair. At the very moment they touched it, bullets flew through the window and hit the wall. They ran away in fear."

I answer with a marvelling smile. I know he wants to believe it.

His three sick children come into my mind. They would be in their mid-forties by now. All of them had multiple sclerosis from the age of ten. All three. They couldn't possibly have survived the war, but I don't dare to ask. Uncle was always reluctant to speak about them, unless my parents inquired with much tact, or unless he could report on something pleasing, a small success of theirs. All three were writers. Sadness was attached to uncle's life, but he never gave it away. I snatched up his story, thread by thread, from adults' quiet words and pieced it together: that he married his cousin—an unusually noble and beautiful woman—and that the close blood relationship was the reason for the children's disability. They divorced later and she married uncle's best friend, a well-known architect who happened to build the villa that uncle commissioned with special facilities to aid the children in their movements.

Since then, he has lived alone in his present condominium with the housekeeper who ran his household. Amalia, the totum factum, was responsible for everything but the dentistry. I had heard about her, but we met only once. Amalia was by his side during the war too, probably helped him to survive in the ghetto in Budapest. Now he tells me in three words: "I married Amalia."

I don't find it strange—maybe I even acquiesce comfortably to the old status quo—that he doesn't call her in to meet me. I don't ask further. It would have been stepping out of my habitual role with him to ask questions.

I find that the proper moment arrives to speak about my situation now, having no one else to ask. "I am divorcing Hoffmann Imre," I tell him.

His answer comes promptly. "I never liked him."

I also tell him about Nathan, that I am undecided about what to do, and about the possibility of emigrating overseas.

"It will be better for you in America," he says.

I know from the past what his picture of America is, an image of an idealized place that doesn't fall much short of Disneyland or Hollywood.

———

I suggest to Miki that he come back with me to Germany, but without any positive offer (I don't have one) or promising future there at easy reach. He doesn't give me any answer. I have no convincing arguments for him, especially as he has started a business already. Furthermore, in the summer of 1946 in Hungary, it looks as if the situation will slowly and steadily normalize. And now, after the recent stabilization of the currency, there is even more reason for serious hope. It is true, the Russians are here, but they are hardly noticeable. I have only one opportunity to observe them closely—at the swimming pool in Budapest, which was an elegant spot before the upheaval. I mainly watch the women changing with rough nonchalance, wherever, in or outside of the cabins. They are oblivious to the natural bulges in their bathing suits.

I also catch scenes on the street, which perhaps other Hungarians refuse to see, or are used to and consider a natural residue of war. From time to time, I glimpse a long line of men and women, dressed as if they were going about their own business—men with attaché cases, women with baskets on their arms coming from the market. They have been picked up at random, to be accused of a crime that will be created once they have been deposited in prison. At the front of the line, a Russian soldier leads them, and another follows at the tail. Maybe those who see these groups think it doesn't concern them; they are only offenders of the law being caught.

One afternoon as I am about to cross the Margaret Bridge, a Russian soldier grabs my arm and starts to pull me. This, I feel, is the beginning of a catastrophe, but then he gets into an argument with his comrade and forgets about me for a second. I take a chance and run away. Maybe I am oversensitive, maybe people who live here see the situation more realistically, but I want to leave. Uncle Mano's words support my belief that emigrating is the right thing to do, though I don't feel able to go into the world alone and without a friend. I retain the thought that Ditta will come with me, even though I haven't spoken to her yet. I am relying on the past. We grew up together and were always together and very close. She has no one closer than me in Hungary, and she always considered me competent in the past.

I travel with Miki to Győr, where we take the run-down bus to Szemere on an equally run-down road. The jolting ride doesn't let me be aware of anything besides the effort of somehow staying on the broken seat. The frequent stops, unloading more and more passengers, make the bus lighter, and it bumps higher on every pothole. Beside the normal season's wear, the road has been sadly abused by all kinds of transports, including tanks, during the war years. It has never been repaired. To begin with, it was not a highway, having only basalt stones on its surface for moderate peacetime use. It was very easily kept in shape by one designated man from town, who took care of it with his single shovel. He took basalt stones from the pile at the roadside, and filled the holes after the spring or autumn rains. It seems the chaos is not over yet. People cannot find their roles to take care of petty jobs like that.

We get off at the edge of Szemere, where the bus leaves us; it continues on with much racket, blowing up dry dust on the road to the next town. I put my foot down on the ground. Automatically I do it, as if I have been doing it daily. At the same time, it is as if I don't know Szemere. I have never been here before without coming home. Step by step, with empty anticipation, I get closer to the house. I don't look left, don't look right, don't look for neighbours, don't want to see anybody I know. I am not angry, I don't carry a grudge. I am still only sad and amazed that it was all allowed to happen. Above all, I don't want questions, either real or pretended ones. I dread being hurt.

I see, getting closer to the house, how maltreated it appears. The gates are wide open into the yard. I walk in, but I don't fall down to the ground as I imagined I would if I ever lived to see it again. I step into the house. In the corridor, I walk by the rooms without a single glance through the windows. There is none of the piled-up furniture we left in my room. There is no cobalt vase with dried lilacs in it that I thought would greet us when we returned. Three families live in the house, people from Szemere. I don't ask why they moved in. There must be some things left, not stolen yet, but I am afraid to find anything familiar. I am not looking for dead objects. What would I do if I found things? I can't take anything on the trip. I can't leave anything to irreverent hands. Better I don't know that it exists, because I would reject selling anything. I feel that nothing I could find could be measured in money.

As I stand in the backyard, a little black dog appears from somewhere. I look at him. He stands, unattached but close. I rest my gaze on him for awhile. Then I realize he is our little black sheepdog. I call his name, "Bogar!" He lifts his sad, black eyes slowly at me. We look at each other for a long time, calmly and quietly. I wish I could read his thoughts. Does he recognize me? We look, we look. But we can't communicate.

On the way to Ivan's, we pass our ex-gardener's dwelling. Through the open window I happen to see the Gobelin picture (a copy of Tiziano's *Lavinia*). I made it as a surprise for my mother. I act as if I haven't seen it, just walk by. I have no room in me for more memories. I don't want empty substitutes from the past.

We find Ivan in his grandmother's house. She, like the rest of the family, didn't return. We meet unsurprised, unimpressed, without excitement. We don't inquire about each other's lives or how we made it through the war. We miss noticing the miracle of being together. We don't know how to begin together again. We are not big enough to fill the empty spaces, the spaces of the people who vanished from our lives. I miss their vital wisdom. The present seems unreal. Or is it only me?

Ditta arrives the same day. We spend the night in Szemere. Ivan accommodates all three of us somehow until the next day, when Miki, Ditta and I go back to Budapest through Győr. After I inquire about Gyula and Anna's latest address, I want to return to Győr again soon.

I begin to outline to Ditta my future plans, my return to Germany, the possibility of emigration overseas later on. I speak about our future as though we will definitely be together. It is the only way I know to begin a new life. I treat it as an established fact that she will come with me. Our friendship lasted through adolescence until fate parted us in war. We complemented each other's missing traits and we never had the ambition to outdo each other; rather, we helped one another if needed. So we start to make plans.

She stays a few days in Budapest, and we use this time to explore the city, the dream city of her life. We visit different memorable spots at her suggestion, including the Danube Promenade. It is late afternoon when we get there. The lights are just going on, one by one, in the dusk when, at last, we reach the chain bridge on the Pest side. We stop and look over the Danube to its opposite shore, where the Buda hills rise, to the illuminated spots on the hillside. We lean against the pillar on the bridge as the kayaks slide noiselessly underneath, and gaze at Budapest's postcard view, its most characteristic face. Ditta is suddenly very quiet. Her stare goes far away. I don't expect tears. I have hardly ever seen her really crying, and I am alarmed now, as tears are running down her face.

"You mean I'll never see that again?" she says.

I have no answer. I don't know myself whether there will be a road back here again.

I don't try any further convincing. I leave it with her, with what I have already said, assuring her of the small possibilities within my reach, comparing our situation with that of the many longing Hungarians who lack a starting address outside the country. Also, I explain, it is realistic to keep in mind that there is hardship ahead until we eventually get to our ultimate destination, but we can only begin with a sensible-looking start. The most important thing is that we will be together, and never alone. I leave it with her, with a slight eagerness. I rely on my memories of her from the past: that she always had trust in me, that she sometimes cried, but only in a brief moment of sentimentality. She never wasted energy on useless brooding; she wiped away her sorrows as soon as she decided to do so.

The next day, I am not surprised when we go on as if there were never a weak moment. I travel back with her to her cousin's place, where we will start our crucial move, travelling illegally back across the Hungarian-Austrian border. Conveniently, she lives in a border town. With the help of well-informed people, we arrange a meeting with a taxi driver who has a connection with a farmer whose land spans the border. These two, temporary business partners, will help us over to the other side. We agree on the date, on the time and on the cost of the operation.

Then, once more on my way to Budapest, I make my planned stopover to visit Gyula and Anna in Győr. They have stayed the way I cherished them in my memory; sweet, naturally tender, stable human beings. It seems that they knew more about what awaited us when we left Szemere than we did. I have the feeling they expected me back, more than anybody else, I guess as a consequence of my youth. I am aware that I should give some explanation as to how it happened, but I can't talk about it. They notice and respect my reticence, turning to events I couldn't have known about. They tell me first about the hidden iron jewellery box in the garden. We believed nobody saw when we buried it there the night before we left. Apparently, the night hid spying eyes. Gyula and Anna watched the digging in our garden for a few nights with apprehension. Then they decided to take it in—they were better guardians—and keep it for us before it got stolen. They handed it over to my brother when he returned. Their other endeavour is revealed when Anna gives me some linen left in my mother's linen closet. To be able to keep it for us, mixed in with her own, she embroidered over my mother's monograms. Now, along with a complete service for twenty-four persons, she returns it to me. Amazed, I look at the beautiful dishes that belonged to my grandmother. I decide to sell them, as they were not my mother's. The money comes at a perfect moment. I need it badly for my trip back to Germany.

I stay with them the whole day, while Anna discloses to me the unexpected drama she was involved in not long after we left. When Hungary had got rid of its Jews, it started on the mixed marriages. They sent away the Jewish spouse, along with the children. Anna feared for her children because, though she changed her religion, she is descended from a Jewish family. She was considered Jewish, so she abandoned them and left them with their non-Jewish father.

Now reunited, they live in a decent apartment with the girls, who are close to ten. Anna keeps a very respectable house. Gyula is in his old engineering job. But they don't seem as happy as I expected after the war. They are not sure about the future, about a total change to a Communist regime. They sense it will be bleak. I listen to them, broken-hearted. I know it should be my turn now to help, but how? I can't even start to encourage them to move to the West. A family of four. Who knows, they might not be strong enough for the trial-by-fire of extended hardship that it would take. I say farewell, smiling to make it lighthearted. "Let's keep in touch," I shout back, waving.

Next, my route continues towards Pécs for my goodbye visit. I expect Eszter definitely to be there, but she hasn't come. Hanna and I can't imagine what to think. I stay only a few days, while I gather in my knapsack some little souvenirs from local shops that I'll be able to carry with me when I leave Hungary. Among them are a few books from a secondhand bookstore. Hanna looks at them. "And what is that?" she asks.

"I must have some Hungarian words with me," I say. She looks at me, pulling her eyebrows high like a question mark, as if saying: *And you are maintaining that you are strong enough to leave everything behind and dare not to belong here?*

"I will never forget those words of yours," she says. She gives me a small homemade jam, a piece of bacon for the road. We promise to write and, in spirit, never part.

Back in Budapest, I go to say goodbye to Uncle Mano. He is expecting me, holding a photograph from the time when I was thirteen. He found it, he says, and he wants me to keep it. I would love to have it, but the implication of his gesture is that we will not meet again. I don't want to accept that, or for him to think that I accept it. I don't take the photograph. And then, at last, we say goodbye.

Next day, the day I leave, I see my little uncle appearing, holding his huge, black umbrella over his head in the pouring rain. He doesn't say why he came. He stays only for a short while. I ask him what I always hoped to know: "Uncle Mano, tell me something about your life."

He smiles slightly, deliberately selecting his thoughts before he says, "I was always alone, like you are."

He takes some Swiss francs from his pocket. "Maybe you can use these," he says. Then he takes my hand and kisses it and without another word he leaves quietly.

I say farewell to Miki. I don't even know when we will be able to meet again. Sadly, he can't forgive me for something and I don't know what, though I am searching my soul.

I arrive with my luggage, a suitcase and a knapsack, to find Ditta. She is halfway packed, all ready to leave in the morning. I hand her the pair of shoes she asked me to purchase for her. To my great regret, she doesn't like them. That means I have to keep them and carry their cost, which is too bad because my money is tight enough anyway. Even sharing the cost of being smuggled through the border with Ditta, I will have precious little for the rest of the trip.

Early the next morning, in the slight drizzle typical of the beginning of October, we both wait with our luggage for the taxi on the street. At last it arrives. I put my luggage in and turn to Ditta. Not moving, she says, "I am unable to leave."

"Pardon?"

"I am unable to leave." Her tone is final, her mind made up.

I say nothing. I get in and pay the driver. We speed away.

In Transit

The taxi drives into a Hungarian peasant farmer's backyard. It is the last frontier village on Hungarian soil. Apparently, the farmer anticipates us, as his horse is already harnessed to the wagon and hammering impatiently with his hoof.

I remain on the wagon for the ride across his land, which overlaps into Austria. There, his neighbour, his "business partner" the Austrian peasant, is loading corn onto his wagon. He visibly notices us coming, but keeps on with his work without pause. In the meantime, as instructed by the Hungarian, I have already pulled a peasant woman's outfit over my own and a kerchief on my head, pulled forward onto my face. Then I change wagons. The Austrian takes up his place on the wooden plank next to me on the front seat and drives off. In my disguise, I am supposed to be taken as his wife.

Soon after we set out, I spot the advancing Russian border patrol and become very quiet while he passes us. I breathe more evenly when I notice that he doesn't find me worthy of a second look. It's then I realize how authentic I must appear. I am very much aware of the impossible situation I am in and that this small success is only the beginning of my long road. But for now, as we continue along, I am much relieved. I keep on playing my peasant's part, hoping none of the patrol decides to come back to search through the wagon and find my hidden knapsack and suitcase under the dry, heaped-up corncobs.

My driver takes me across farmland and through the town, and he says nothing all the while. I don't think to converse or ask further questions, as I committed myself to trusting him when I chose to get across to Austria with his assistance. Then, in an instant, he swerves his horse into his backyard and stops in front of the stalls. He instructs me to stay indoors there and show myself in the yard only if I have to visit the outdoor toilet. I find the inside vacant; his beasts must be out grazing. I move further in, to where he left my luggage deep in the semi-darkness. I scan the place with apprehension, the dusty walls, the wet dung, smelling musty and heavy. I am alone. I think about what's next while sitting on my suitcase for the rest of the morning and a good part of the afternoon, until the time arrives for the train to Vienna.

Returning from the washroom at one point, I find his daughter kneeling at my knapsack. Seeing me, she drops whatever she has in her hand and runs out, flushed. What she dropped on the wet straw is the box of talc powder where I have hidden several pieces of my jewellery, the pieces that Anna and Gyula returned. Shocked, I sift through the wet, stamped-down straw to recover what she has left behind. I'm broken by the unexpected incident, but the skilled way she did her job while I was out for only a couple of minutes tells me it would be useless to complain to her father the farmer. I guess looting is included in the package.

He then takes me to the railway station, purchases the ticket to Vienna for me, and I board the train. Shyly, I enter, and keep to myself. I am a foreign body in a train full of Austrians, alienated by an unpredictable environment. I remain silent for the entire trip, anxiously avoiding conversation or involvement. If anyone talks to me, I turn my back as if I haven't heard. One single word in my Hungarian accent would promptly give my identity away. As was the case two months before, I have no legal right to be in Austria, but, just as before, I make it to my destination. This time, Vienna.

Standing on the Vienna platform with my luggage, I do my best to hide how lost I am. Everyone is taking their own belongings and knows where to go, except me. I know only that the Rotchild Hospital is where I want to be.

But which direction to start? I must be careful whom I ask. I have heard about the place by hearsay as the first safe haven, the first rest place for those running from the East to the West. As it turns out, it is a chaotic, dirty place. But now I am approaching it by streetcar and getting as close as possible with my heavy load. At the right stop I work my way down, dragging my luggage. As I am about to lift my suitcase down the stairs, someone reaches over my shoulder to grab it away from me. I turn, astonished, and see two young men, both over six feet tall, running with my luggage along the long block, toward the Rotchild Hospital. Out of breath I run after them, catching up inside its hall, where they are about to deposit my things. They turn, not even leaving me time for a thank-you nod.

I feel instantly in seventh heaven and too eager to interpret this prompt change, this humane welcome as a promising omen. I feel as if I have dropped the past months' heavy burden in seconds and risen above it all. It looks as if the road into the world is unfolding smoothly in front of me. In my good mood I hardly notice the unhappy faces of the recently arrived who stand around fuming in the makeshift office while waiting for assistance. The employees do what they can. They seem to be temporary help, gathered in haste from what was available. In fact I am amazed, when I approach one of the women behind a disarrayed desk for accommodation, that she manages some kind of administration at all, amid the incessant flux of people.

At last I am assigned a bed. It is a shared one, as it turns out. Luckily, my bed mate is a woman, even though she is slightly undignified-looking. But at this point, late in the evening and after such a nerve-wracking day, I would agree to any-

123

thing, just to stretch out. I take my own blanket from my knapsack, roll myself up in it tightly, which lends me some separation, and lie down for the night.

In the middle of my sleep I hear a commotion close to my bed. Unwilling to believe that my rest is already ending, I look up and see two policemen standing at my side interrogating my strange bedfellow. She is ordered to get up. She gets out of bed as she's told, doesn't struggle, simply leaves with them. She seems to know why she's caught. I ask no questions either. Without further wasting my night, I make myself more comfortable and close my eyes to sleep, forgetting her at once. She might be a thief, a harmless eccentric, a murderer, or a Nazi hiding among refugees. In chaotic Europe, yet so close to war, still overturned with its roots exposed, people's appearances are irrelevant. One hopes only to stay out of and away from anybody else's business. Compassion is, of necessity, out of style in 1946. No one can risk being involved with anyone on the go. I accept that for myself, too.

But the bed I sleep in, it turns out, is not my permanent spot either for the time of my stay. I have to get out of it in the morning and sit on my suitcase the entire next day, waiting for something to happen. At night, I am assigned to another room, where men and women are free, without limit or barrier, to sleep on the bare floor. I roll myself in my blanket tightly so I have the illusion of some privacy, in this way separated from the alien craziness around me. But as soon as the lights are out a young man sneaks up to me and wants to rip my blanket off. Luckily, he doesn't succeed, as I am rolled into it like a mummy over and over again. He gives up the fight then, swearing at me in a rage, and remains hostile for the coming days as if he were in the right. I hold on to my blanket as my only friend for my entire trip, especially while I rest and lose my vigilance.

Then, in order to avoid the soup line, and with all the pride of a well-to-do person, I approach a teller in the first bank I can find with the intention of changing my Uncle Mano's

Swiss francs. The teller glances up at me and says, "Out of circulation." I don't want to believe I haven't a cent to my name and have to stand once again, bowl in hand, waiting for the ladle of warm liquid to be thrown into it. It is a reminder of a dreadful picture and the feeling that, if the soup is not enough, there is nowhere to go for more. I feel I am sinking into a hopeless state, doubting and hungry, when luck suddenly strikes. It is not that I manipulate it or position myself cleverly, it just so happens that I am taken by a Zionist group out of the Rotchild and put with a group on its way to Linz, to another camp, one step closer to my goal.

————

As the freight train is just about to pull out of the Vienna station, I notice a leather-jacketed young man in his twenties swinging his small attaché case playfully, approaching the already moving train with leisurely ease. He pulls himself up on the freight wagon with one jaunty step and posts himself next to me. There are no benches; we travel standing up. Unlike the rest of us, he is smiling self-confidently, as if he were from a different breed. He turns his glance around the wagon inquisitively, it seems. When he finishes his inquiry and looks settled, I remark, "How come you travel so light?"

"I had no time to pack more," he tells me. "Actually, I know the route crossing over from Hungary very well. I have come over numerous times with the Russians on army trucks. But this time is my last."

"Have you been caught smuggling?" I ask.

"No, I cleaned my employer's safe out in Budapest. And off I went." He tells me this proudly, as if he had managed a heroic deed.

Shocked, I listen to this real-life thief, the first one I have ever knowingly met. With a mixture of fright and sadness, I turn to the decent-looking young man, thinking him probably lost to bad influence, sinking so low.

"But how can you do that? How can you break into someone's safe?"

"Just clever planning. My employer is the head of the Joint Distribution Committee in Budapest, the charity organization. I asked her for a job, and she took me. She liked me. I became her trusted right hand. She even trusted me with the safe's key. When I found the right day for it, I took the safe's contents and crossed over to Austria." He is smiling as he tells me this.

"How do you feel about misusing her trust? Don't you feel sorry to do that to a person who was so kind to you?"

He laughs. "She did send the police after me, catching me at the Rotchild, ordering me not to move from the spot."

"But you are here now. What will happen?"

"What do you take me for, naive? Ought I to do what they say?"

I try to convince him, as I can see a good upbringing is still somewhere inside him, to find his way back to society. But after a few futile words I realize that he has deep contempt for middle-class thinking and conformity. He thinks working is for fools and suckers. The smart people, the people he admires, are the card sharks and prostitutes. It is for their acceptance he strives.

Still, I make a last attempt to place him in a world I recognize. "But now you have a great chance to start anew."

He laughs, a superior kind of laugh. "My cronies are waiting for me in Linz."

I am disappointed, even sad, to admit that altruism can't work for everyone, especially not for someone who doesn't know its meaning. But who knows? Maybe we are both right to a degree.

Later, at the end of the trip when we get off the train, I realized that my only comb is gone from my purse. He has stolen it.

———

The camp in Linz is a primitive dwelling, but not nearly as dirty and worn as the Rotchild. It consists of a number of oblong-shaped barracks, each divided into two large rooms with cots. Coming inside from the cold rain, I feel pleasantly cosy being in a heated place. I put my stuff on an empty cot, which I guess will be mine for an unknown length of time. I realize, amazed, that men and women share rooms. Having no better option, I adjust myself to going to bed fully dressed, then undressing under the cover of my blanket. The same routine happens in the morning, only in reverse. I get out from under the covers fully dressed. Nevertheless, aggressors appear from nowhere. Especially frightening after dark is the road to the shower or washrooms; both are outdoors.

It is late autumn, and during my four weeks in Linz the rain never stops. It turns the unpaved soil into a liquid mass. It becomes a problem, requiring firm resolution, to go to the outdoor facilities, as the sticky clay oozes up into my shoes.

Here again I must rely on the food supply from camp, which is very meagre. Linz has a steady daily menu: boiled noodles mixed with fried onions. That is all my nourishment. By the end of my stay I can't even bear the smell of it. I am sure the difference between what we eat and what we are supposed to eat finds its way into someone's deep, selfish pocket.

As weeks and weeks pass, I can't see a way out of Linz. I wait for some possible chance, but nothing encouraging happens. I think about the young man in Salzburg for whose parents I took the American cigarettes to Hungary; he could probably help me on the road again. Salzburg is close and feasible, yet I can't see how to move on, since I haven't got a cent of my own. Reluctantly, as a last resort, I write to my cousin there to request that he mail me twenty dollars so I can purchase a train ticket.

A reply comes very soon, but from his sister, who has married an American army officer stationed in Salzburg. She explains that her brother has left for Palestine, but she encloses the twenty dollars.

With much difficulty, I find my way to the train station in Linz, and after a couple of hours I arrive in Salzburg on a raw November day, already in darkness. I am unprepared, without appropriate clothing and shivering with cold, but I have arrived. I make my way to my cousin's sublet apartment. The owner lets me in. I find my cousin in her room, standing at the glazed tile-oven. Glancing at me, she exclaims, "These Raabs are driving me crazy."

I search for words, after her curious non-welcome. "Why, how many do you have?"

"Your brother just left yesterday," she says.

"What?" I can't believe what she just said. "But he didn't want to come with me. I can't understand it."

"Well, apparently he changed his mind. The hotel called me today to ask what to do with the stuff he left in his room."

The next day I go to his hotel. I get the key to his room and, sure enough, find his coat hanging on the closet door and his boots, shoes and the rest of his clothes inside the closet. All sadly abandoned: these beautiful treasures, so difficult to obtain after the war. I fold my hands in dismay. Then I pack his suitcase and knapsack, hoping for miraculous strength, since from now on I have to carry two suitcases and two knapsacks, his and mine.

———

My next plan is to meet the man with whom I exchanged the false travelling papers for cigarette smuggling. But his message is that he doesn't want to see me again. I can't believe it at first, but through a third person he lets me know clearly that I "didn't deliver the full load to his parents." I have no words to express my feelings. Until now I have reflected proudly on my accomplishment, and now his anger hits me like a thunderbolt.

I try to think, and begin to trace back my moves. When I left for Pécs, I entrusted the parcel to the people I stayed with in Budapest. I asked them to hand the tightly wrapped and roped box over to his parents when they came to claim it. That is the only time when something could have happened. What a fool. No lesson is harsh enough to convince me to give up believing in humanity. I can't even prove my innocence. How can I convince him? But what difference does it make who took it? I add this to my not-so-great memories of Budapest. I have lost my contact, which I need, because Salzburg is not Germany, where I want to go.

As fast as possible, I try to forget the whole incident and get busy planning how I can move on, as I don't intend to stay one more day at my cousin's. I look up the Zionist headquarters in Salzburg and arrive there just before a whole convoy of trucks, filled with eventual immigrants to Palestine, starts out for Munich, Germany.

The energetic young men who put the transport together don't ask me for any identification or papers, not even whether I am a Zionist or not. The only passport valid to them is "a Jew in need." They take me.

I don't ask questions, neither does anyone with the transport. We pile on the trucks, expecting that nothing will be easy. Inside, we are filled with the emigrant's tension; outside, we exhibit controlled calm, like patients before surgery in a hospital.

In the middle of the night we reach the German border. Our leaders, with fantastic adroitness, negotiate and respond to Austrian, German and American patrols, while we sit silently, not knowing what the conversation is about.

At about two in the morning, we make a stopover for a few hours' rest at a concrete tower, seemingly a wartime bunker. Apparently, we can't leave our luggage on the truck; everything has to be carried up to the bunker. We are trudging up the narrow staircase, me with the two knapsacks and two suitcases, dragging ourselves up to the fourth floor. I take two of my packs up a few stairs while leaving two behind and then pick them up alternately. While I toil away on the sparingly lit stairs, a man picks up one of the bags and carries it way up to the fourth floor. I find the gesture unexpected, in the present "no thought for others" environment, and I tell him so.

Arriving at last with everything, I throw myself on a free cot, my whole body throbbing, desperately wondering how I will repeat the task in reverse the next morning. I stretch out and close my eyes and eventually calm down, only to become aware of someone sitting on my cot, stroking me. I open my eyes to see the same man who helped me out by carrying a suitcase. In deep disgust, without saying a word, I kick him off my cot. The incident leaves me embittered. I can't get to sleep, thinking about how not to say thanks for a favour with a smile, and how to judge hidden calculations in benevolence. I would love to talk to other women around here, but can't see anyone alone like me.

———

I part company with the transport in Munich and find quarters in the museum, which has been opened up for transient travellers. There again, I share a room, or rather a hall, with many, but know no one. No food is provided, so I am left to look for my own. Though I am very careful and my food is only barely enough, I know that soon the twenty dollars will come to an end. I dread the thought, because I feel I am getting close to a state of exhaustion. The effect of the last four months has begun to wear me out physically and mentally. Even when I get to Westfalen I cannot count on permanence in any way, but at least I will be able to close the same door behind me every night. Nor do I harbour hopes that the place I will eventually call home, and dare to love, somewhere, sometime, is anywhere close to me yet.

Naturally, I think of Nathan, though we haven't exchanged letters since I left in June. I didn't want to be disturbed in making my decision to leave Hungary. I want to depend only on my own judgment. I know he is waiting for me, and my uncertain return, unless I choose differently and let him know that. Actually, throughout my wandering months, beset by conflicts, dealing with my memory of the deceased, with the pain of farewell to friends and doubt in my future, when all seemed hopeless and unbearable, he was the sole reassuring constant I could think of. And now, if I let him know my whereabouts, he would come to meet me. But amazingly, being that close, I hesitate. If only I had a friend. If only I had a wise friend, someone to talk to, to help me clear my mind, help me decide. I feel I can't endure much more. And when my last dollars are gone I will be left without even the option of sending a letter to Nathan. I arrive at the end of my resistance and make the move. After the letter is mailed, I feel better.

Having reached out, I don't dare to move from the spot in case he arrives. A few days later, Nathan finds me waiting in the museum, sitting on my cot. One glance at his honest, trustworthy face, a friend's face, and I break down, overcome by the last four months' memories. I let go of my remaining strength and let it sink like snowflakes into a winter coat in a heated room. It feels as if a shelter has grown around me. Nathan's face lights up with a smile upon seeing me. He welcomes me kindly in his natural manner. He has been wisely and calmly expecting me all these months. Suddenly, I am eager to talk. My long-restrained words pour out. I can hardly stop, believing I have arrived. I can't bear not to believe I have arrived at the end of my wandering.

Waiting

A new chapter in my life begins at the end of November 1946. I finally arrive in Nathan's family apartment in Westfalen. His sister Frimetka and her husband, and his brother Shmulek and his wife, welcome me as if I were a long-absent family member finally returned. Frimetka, seeing me, says, "I have been waiting here impatiently, because I know Nathan is bringing somebody worth waiting for."

After we spend the first night in their apartment, with a real sense of hospitality, a prepared breakfast awaits us. She even makes coffee for me. Her gesture indicates to me her effort and her will to understand the differences between our cultures, hers and mine, and that she is ready to cross that bridge.

"You'll be surprised. I made coffee for you," she tells me.

She certainly does surprise me, although not entirely in the way she means to. I can hardly restrain my surprise about what I see in front of me, coffee grounds swimming in my cup of hot milk. But I recognize her work and offer the expected result: my appreciation. I drink it with a straight face. Poles are avid tea drinkers, and, as I find out much later, if they ever have coffee this is the way they make it.

Beginning with that first morning in their kitchen, among kind, good-hearted people, I feel at ease. It feels like home. I know the reality of the outside world, the surroundings, the uncertainties, but I can't bear to bring it from my subconscious mind. Here, in their busy, warm kitchen, it is like an island of safety for me.

I am tired, I am longing for permanence. If I allow myself to dream of the future I see myself in tranquillity, peacefully settled on some spot on earth, devoting my life to my future family. Nathan and I decide to marry in the beginning of 1947.

But before that, just a few days after my arrival, in the middle of the night, my brother Miki knocks at my door. I am surprised only by the unexpected timing of his arrival. Otherwise, I knew when I picked up his luggage in the hotel room in Salzburg that he would eventually find his way to me. Where else would he go? The next day he gets registered, and a room is provided for him in the village.

––––––––

As before, it is not easy to find decent living quarters. The village, the place of our enfranchisement, is still overcrowded, as only a few have managed to leave or emigrate. Nathan and I settle in with his family. That makes six in the apartment. A new addition comes later: his brother's wife has a new baby boy, a wonderful fresh life, precious to all of us, even to others outside the family. A first wonder amid a sadly childless community.

Virtually nothing has changed since my first day in town. For over two years we have been in the same situation: the distributed food and the second-hand clothing. As much as we have had enough of the handouts and long to exchange our empty existence for a productive life with a purpose, we are not able to move from this spot. We are wasting the best years of our lives. After years of war, we are forced to wait idly for a miracle, hoping some country will eventually take us in, but we have no say in it. We will have to begin again, without money, without skills, without language.

The United Nations Relief and Rehabilitation Administration (UNRA) and the Joint Distribution Committee (JOINT) share the cost of emigration for us D.P.s (displaced persons). But I have no connection in America or Canada. Even if I had, their immigration policy looks hopeless for most of us. Their first requirement for applicants is to have a close relative there, a parent, a child, a brother or sister. If you are lucky, and have a relative, it can still take years to get there, as a result of the strict quota system, which has remained unaltered since before the war. The Hungarian and Polish quotas are the worst and are desperately overdrawn, and always were, even before the war. Ironically, the best is the German quota. As if they were the ones entitled to start a new life. The Western European countries, those closest to us, like France, Belgium and England, don't consider letting D.P.s in.

Palestine is one dangerous possibility for getting out of Germany. We think about it, but can't decide. The route entails being smuggled in by boats or small ships, but it's impossible to get there unnoticed by the British coastguard. Once boats are discovered, fierce battles follow on Palestine's Mediterranean shore. Predictably, the would-be immigrants lose. The British fight them back to sea, or ban them to Cyprus, the British colony, to be locked up for an undetermined time on the island. Hardly the dream of those recently freed from a German concentration camp.

A trickle of legal immigrants are accepted and allowed by the British into Palestine. Considering the mass of aimless people in Europe, the number is a drop in the ocean. Shmulek's wife has a sister there, her only living relative. They hope to be let in sometime when the baby is old enough to endure such a trip. Shmulek appears silently reluctant when their move to Palestine comes up. He doesn't seem in a hurry to go. Maybe he doesn't want to part from his family. Maybe he feels he has been through enough already.

He and Nathan start buying and selling things together. It is just a small activity to keep busy, I think. At first, I can't understand what it is all about. Naively, I don't inquire what they buy and where they sell, as if that part were out of my territory. Only later do I begin to associate myself with their thinking: they are trying to accumulate some minimum financial holding in order to begin a life outside of Germany.

I find the distributed food and used clothes I wear adequate. The possibility of buying new things does not enter my mind. It is as if I have forgotten normal dealings, as if I didn't know any better. Otherwise, I act out the routine the way I learned in the past. Automatically, I search for an interest, for something purposeful to do, but as much as I was always in the middle of a book before, now I don't search out books. Without knowing why, I act with the underlying feeling: "What for? It is only temporary." Only once, I stumble over one, an 800-page book in German, about the early Middle Ages in Sweden. I read it tenaciously but I don't strive to store its information.

———

I establish a connection with Hanna again. In her first letter she tells me that I missed Eszter by two weeks. She arrived after I left Hungary. She was detained by the Americans, who caught her crossing the German border into Austria and imprisoned her with Steve for two months in Salzburg. Poor Eszter. I was so lucky. But at last she has peace at Hanna's. She adds her own few lines to Hanna's letter, but writing is not her strength.

My correspondence with people who knew me from before lends the only permanence I have. I write to a few, and also to Ditta, though regrettably in my eyes our friendship has lost its original lustre. The tone of my letters to her, unintentionally, is reserved and distant, since our parting has disturbed my flawless memories of her. Still, I am compelled to hold on to whatever is left. I avoid thinking about our last-minute parting, but it remains a painful memory. I do send letters to others, most importantly to Uncle Mano and Hanna.

It is usually a quiet time when I sit down at the kitchen table to write to them. Then I am relaxed enough to put words after words on paper—to friends. I tell my thoughts with full trust that they will understand. Then I begin to wait with anticipation for their replies, and when at last they arrive their words give me a sense of reality from my old world, the only real world: from the uncle who influenced and enriched my child's life and who has known me from the beginning; from my other friend, who has known me from the beginning of my growing-up years, from the start of my life. They write to the authentic me, to the person who was me, who now seems to be lost, or can only be found by real friends.

———

Meanwhile, the world outside Germany goes on, leaving me behind. It floats by on self-congratulatory waves, exuding a spirit of "a job well done." The war is won. The world is newly born. It embraces inevitable changes with optimism. New orders, new views, new politics, with which I'm afraid I will never catch up, being isolated in an incidental backwater in Westfalen. Maybe I don't want to catch up. Maybe I want to stay a stranger, holding on to my memories, my last remaining possessions.

People here, in the after-war world, all have memories from the past. And that is all they have. What is lost, what is wiped out, is their tangible past. It is gone without leaving a trace; often not as much as a messenger is left. But people remember the past and speak about it. The listeners here are listening with their own painful memories, incapable of sympathy for others. And who knows what is real, imagined, or a dream come true in the process of remembering. I don't entrust my past to doubting, callous ears, to profane words. I don't want to rid myself easily of my pain. I want to *bury it with piety*, individually, so I keep it alive *under my own unconditional care*.

———

In the first winter months of 1947, it looks as if we have been forgotten under the frozen snow in our D.P. camp in Westfalen. It feels as if no joy will ever again come to us. We hear about the few who have received affidavits, but we don't know anyone who has moved yet. Nobody has heard about the Commission which came some time ago from Canada, looking for seamstresses. I didn't sign up for the interview when it was announced, thinking, "I am not a seamstress." It turns out later that women who knew only how to hold a needle signed on. They were smarter than me. I hear they have been accepted, but that is all they know.

While nothing seems to be going our way, I search my memory for connections. My grandmother's brother's address in Buenos Aires, Argentina, pops into my mind. I write at once to let him know we survived, my brother and myself, and that we are in Germany. At the same time, I hint at the idea of an affidavit to Argentina. With a positive feeling, I mail my letter, thinking that if the address is correct, his answer can't be anything but affirmative. There are only a few of our family left.

After waiting weeks, at last I hold his reply in my hand. He is very happy to know we are well and alive, but he is not in a position to help us out. His blunt refusal catches me unprepared, but I do my best to look at it objectively. After all, I do understand him, and also the many others overseas who don't want to disturb their own comfort, maybe even their achieved status by bringing in someone from their old, forgotten world. At the same time, I admire and appreciate those few who are brave enough to take a risk by taking in unknown people, even if they are distant relatives. In reality, we don't suffer physically in Germany. We have shelter, and enough food to get by. It is only the uselessness of our lives that eats away at us.

Many strive to reestablish ties with relatives overseas. Frimetka's husband doesn't sit motionless, either. One day he surprises us by holding a letter from a cousin of his in America. As a distant relative, he writes, he can't bring them to America, but while he looked into different avenues, he found someone in Ecuador, South America, who is ready to provide the necessary papers for them.

Shortly afterwards, as unreal as it sounded at first, it comes about. The papers arrive, and their departure follows unexpectedly fast. They leave by train to Paris, then to Le Havre, from where everyone seems to sail.

I say farewell with some envy, while Frimetka says, apprehensively, "Who knows where we are going and what lies ahead. Will I see my brothers again?" She adds, "If I ever arrive, I'll leave no stone unturned to take you out of here."

Taking comfort from her thought, I take a chance and dare to ask her to include my brother, his wife and their baby girl in her plan. I know she will understand my bold request, being herself so close to her own family.

———

A few short months later, Shmulek's wife loses patience and talks him into the trip to Palestine. They leave. The apartment feels big and quiet with only Nathan and myself left, alone for the first time. After Shmulek's departure I see a lull in Nathan's energy. It is as if he has lost his confidence, as if he feels incomplete without his brother. Being with him all these years, side by side, he misses his strong, younger brother, the youngest and boldest who was the last in the family and somehow remained a source of youth.

Nathan was used to Shmulek's presence throughout the war years, from the entrainment to Mauthausen—where convicts (*die Häftlinge*) arrived with the tag *untauglich* (unfit, useless) written on their foreheads—to when Nathan got to the point where he had no strength to walk anymore and Shmulek concealed him from the guard and saved him from being shot on the spot by dragging him to work and back to the barracks at night, laying him out on his cot. At the time Nathan felt he must be at the end. He pleaded with his brother, "It's no use, leave me here, I can't move anymore." The next morning, Shmulek came running, shouting, "The Americans are here, Nathan, Nathan, we are saved." Then Shmulek began to carry food to him, whatever he could find, and fed him back to strength.

Now, Nathan tries to cope without Shmulek but doesn't dare venture into anything wholeheartedly. He is waiting to hear from him. He follows the Jewish paper, which from time to time arrives in camp, and eagerly reads the political news about Palestine, hoping for peace when his brother gets there.

Nathan doesn't know the future. He doesn't know that a few months later in the Métro in Paris he will overhear two Jewish men in conversation. "Did you hear that Shmulek G. was killed in Tel Aviv by shrapnel?" Nathan will grab the man's coat in anguish shouting, "Talk, man, I am his brother." But the men will know nothing more, and Nathan will come stumbling back to our hotel room and throw himself down in pain.

―――――

I keep busy with my duties in my primitive household, like cooking on the woodstove, which I don't mind at all. While I work I routinely turn on the old radio in the wintry kitchen, to Radio-Luxembourg. It is noon when their daily program begins and it always starts with a women's singing contest. It starts just about when I do the last adjustment, steaming up the window by stirring the warm lunch, ready to serve it. Every day it is the same: a woman's mirthful, lilting voice, sounding as if it were from the audience, singing "La vie en rose." Cheering and applause follow until the next woman comes on, again singing cheerfully, "La vie en rose." I can't grasp why there is jubilation over the singing, but it sure sounds happy and uncomplicated. It sounds easy and promising, as if times were settled again. As if all the residue and the aftermath of war were fading away. As if we could begin life anew.

Nathan and I spend our days in harmony. He listens to my thoughts and supports my dreams. That alone helps me to find a relative balance, a hint of security. We accept each other's ambitions, trust each other's judgments and we share a mutual respect. Interestingly so, since we come from different countries, from different milieux, upbringings and backgrounds. But the basic ingredient in our relationship is provided by our common principles in life, which are valid anywhere, in any society.

I see babies and children appearing in camp and I begin to think about starting a family. I share more and more the view of those who dare to have children, that the present simple lifestyle adapts itself well to staying home and caring for babies. Who knows what the future holds out in the world? I see a chance to reach for a beginning, for a commitment and a purpose. Nathan goes about indifferently, without comment, but I don't give too much thought to that. I believe I can read his mind. "This is the woman's department." I feel happier than I have in years and, being so close to my goal, I don't pay attention to anything else.

But then the unbelievable happens. In the fifth month of my pregnancy, Nathan has to take me unexpectedly to the hospital. During the forty-kilometre ride in the taxi, I shun doubts, as if my cup were filled to the top with bad luck, and more bad luck would be unfair.

It is a D.P. hospital, the only one in the area where we have the right to go for treatment. The staff, the doctors and the nurses are ex-SS men and women, serving under forced penalty. Nathan leaves me there and returns to camp. I apprehensively follow the nurse into a spacious room where she points wordlessly to a bed. I feel a terrible accusation in her hard look. Her gesture towards the bed is like motioning an annoying nuisance away.

I do what I am told, but nobody comes to look after me. Nobody comes to ask why I am there. I am alone except for a teenaged girl at the far end of the room. For the rest of the day and night, no one answers my urgent calls. No one is alerted, later, by my screams of terror. I have to bring my dead baby into the world by myself, and in front of the young girl. The nurse comes in the morning to take it away.

I am packed up without a word and wheeled into the surgery in the morning. The doctor looks at me and says, "What did you do to yourself?"

I wake up back in the room in bed. There I am kept, completely overlooked by nurse and doctor, as if I didn't exist, for eight days. My bloody sheet from the birth is never changed, and it doesn't come into my mind that I deserve better.

I learn a few foreign words as they come echoing from distant rooms through the hospital's cold corridors. The most piercing are the beseeching calls of a Polish child: "Boli! Boli!" ("It hurts! It hurts!")

———

Nathan takes me back from the hospital to our place. I am expecting a remark or a comment or some reference to my miscarriage but, curiously, he remains silent. I guess he considers it a minor event compared to all the losses we and others have already had to deal with over the last six years. But it was my first testing into life. It would have been nice to hear a sign or token of sympathy. Yet the sympathy doesn't come, not from him, not from others I know. So I just seal it off, away from everyone, discouraged from ever openly expressing pain.

————

At first it is hard to get involved in life's routine as if nothing had happened. A transition comes only gradually, and I begin to realize that my way out is the road onward. In my search for a "time being" purpose, I find the need for some spring clothing and I sort through my second-hand clothes. I take them to a seamstress, Matild. I knew her from Győr and now, since camp, she has become a friend. Matild loves to socialize and talk, enjoys company, keeping an open house for anyone to drop in. Everybody is welcome at her place for a short chat or a longer afternoon stay while she happily sews away, holding the piece she just happens to be working on in her lap and taking an eager part with her strong definitive voice in the conversation. And I, with her hearty instructions, turn distributed second-hand clothes into more appealing garments, fixed as if they were really made for me. The activity at least releases me from the constant good-for-nothing feeling, the mood I have been in since my fiasco.

Still, the most contented time for me during this period is writing to faraway friends. Whenever I am ready for solitary conversation, I put my thoughts on paper, keeping my friends close to me through the mail. Then, every time I see an envelope with my name and address, their reply, I am surprised that it arrived, and look upon it as God's wonder coming from normal times. In my mind, the Europe of 1947 is not normal times. I see Europe as a helter-skelter place, unsettled, unsorted, irresponsible, unguided and cruel, where nobody cares what happens to the next being. I have difficulty believing that old values have emerged from the ruins of society, that a skeleton of old order still functions. Or if it does, it is habit, not love, that makes it operate. That is how I see it in 1947, adrift, belonging nowhere.

I go through my days with a sense of waiting for something to happen, a condition that has become habitual. Since the onset of war, I have been waiting for its end, to continue life without the manacle of fear and uncertainty. Now, I am waiting for some nameless relief. I am waiting in milk lines, in food lines, in clothing lines, or for some chance to turn up. While I am waiting I do nothing lasting or significant. I do everything transiently, superficially, with not much heart in it, to match the way I see the world. Anything I do, I do impatiently, yet passively, without putting myself into it. I am waiting with suspense for real life to begin.

Nathan is also waiting. He is expecting a letter from his sister, since her last postcard came from France before they even left Europe, and for news from his brother. We continue waiting and hoping, watching daily for the mailman. The day comes at last. We can hardly believe it. A letter reaches us from afar, from Ecuador.

We read it again and again, imagining the marvel of being in Ecuador, but unable really to picture it. One thing I remember about Ecuador from my school days is the name of its highest snow-covered peak, Chimborazo. In school, instead of saying (when we wanted to express something enormous), "this is the top, it is the most," we said, "this is its Chimborazo." Now, I find this coincidence funny, almost eerie, but I keep it to myself. Who here would find it worth a smile?

Frimetka tells us that she is expecting a baby and that her husband has got a job at a milk-processing plant. He himself adds a few words: "I feel like at home." I don't know what that means. They are lodged temporarily in a small hotel, and they have met other Jewish emigrants, mostly Germans. I find her letter could have been from anywhere in Europe, whereas I expected to read about some peculiarity of Quito, the capital of Ecuador, where they now are.

Finishing the letter, I study the alien air-mail envelope closely. It is mauve with a striped purple-yellow border. On the stamp is a bright, peacock-like tropical bird, holding his small head on his long neck vigilantly high, as if on watch, while he spreads his tail-feathers proudly. An odd but pleasing strangeness surrounds the whole thing, which I can't label at first, until I compare it in my mind to its European counterpart. Here in Europe, mail services are regarded, stiffened with tradition, with unquestionable respect. Nothing frivolous is possible on a stamp. The only imaginable picture can be of a national hero. The Ecuadorian envelope gives a playful impression, as if they wouldn't take themselves so dead-seriously. It pleases me.

Soon after the first, a second letter comes with the great news that a sponsor has been found in Ecuador for us, and also for my brother and his family. Now, I can suddenly hope for more than just exploring the envelope. I can visualize a glimpse of a new life. Only Nathan looks worried, apprehensive of starting out in a new country. But I feel, once free, I'll master any problem. Besides, I don't expect much, only a modest, down-to-earth lifestyle.

That is how I see it from Germany.

Farewell

In August of 1948, after close to five years have been taken out of our lives in Germany, we pack our meagre suitcases and leave for Paris to pick up our visas at the Ecuadorian consulate. My brother and his family come too.

The JOINT (the Jewish relief organization) accommodates us in a small hotel in the rue Doudauville, in the fifteenth Arrondissement. The room is about eleven feet by ten feet, has one bed, an armoire, a tiny washbasin and the ubiquitous bidet, placed in a prominent spot. Characteristically, there is no bath. I indulge in the luxury of a public bath, not far away, once a week. There is one toilet, if it can be so called, outside in the corridor, for the use of the whole floor. At first sight it is unbelievable. It is a hole in the floor, on its left and right side is an imprint outlining the form of a shoe, indicating where to stand . . . and then, one had better practise the procedure of jumping out into the corridor before one is flushed with toilet water up to one's ankles.

The bedroom has a window overlooking where the hotel backyard is supposed to be, but instead there is only a crowd of overlapping roofs. In the unrelenting August heat I go to the open window for a breeze and that is how I discover one of the favourite meeting places of the Parisian rats, picnicking undisturbed on the rooftops. They enjoy the people's habit of nonchalantly flinging garbage out the windows.

At night, when at last I decide to go to bed, I leave the light on for fear of the bedbugs. I would rather tolerate the beam of light from the naked bulb in the ceiling than the bugs. I soon learn that they love to creep out of hiding in the dark; thinking to myself, *what happens, happens*, I leave the light on for the night. Somehow, though, our light is off each morning. I don't research the matter further; later, I become better acquainted with the Parisian hotel owner's habit of controlling all the rooms' lights from the cubicle downstairs. But he never exchanges a word with me about it; I continue to leave it on and he continues to turn it off.

The JOINT provides one warm meal daily, and that is lunch, on the rue Richet, where we meet many who are, like ourselves, in transit. Serving a square meal for so many is an almost impossible task. The portions are small, but the baguettes are limitless. I have never eaten so much bread in my life. In the evening a *lamp d'alcool* serves to warm up a can of something in the hotel.

We happily explore Paris during our first days. I have the advantage of a seasoned guide beside me: Nathan, who visited Paris twice before the war. We walk on the Grand Boulevard, he teaches me how to commute on the Métro, we take a glance at the Louvre, we stroll at the Jardins du Luxembourg and marvel at the Place de la Concorde. He even discovers a few old friends. In the summer of 1948, we feel confident and positive.

———

After a week in Paris I decide to join the illegal work force, to make a few francs. Nathan also looks for work, but for men it is not that easy.

I start my career as a *finisseuse*, sewing hemlines, buttons, loops for belts, and finishing dresses inside. My first day on the job, I put the dress comfortably in my lap and start to sew its hem the way I remember doing it in Matild's place in Germany. Madame Juri, the boss, gives me one glance. "Madame," she says, "with your kind of sewing you won't take much home at the end of the week."

From then on I speed through the days, 7 a.m. to 5 p.m., working faster than possible. I realize just how fast, as occasionally Madame Juri folds the finished dresses and is left with a few dropped buttons in her hand.

In spite of the hardship, poor nutrition and wretched housing, I fall in love with Paris. It makes me instantly feel at ease, as if I have been here before, as if I were in Budapest before the war. I feel free, as if it were home, and never think about the frequent obligatory trips to the cold *prefecture* (police station) to renew our permit to stay. In spite of its bureaucrats, everyone feels free on the streets of Paris; accepted and unjudged, however one happens to be.

As I squeeze out from the Métro shoulder-to-shoulder with workers like me, the streets are still empty. It is 7 a.m. in the Paris that ordinary tourists don't get to see. I feel almost an insider as I pass the beggars, the rubbish-can pickers and the rag collectors as they alternate with each other, rummaging in cans at each doorway. Unconcerned about me, they go on, engrossed in their own business. I am ignored, unworthy of their glance. I try to slide by, as flat as I can make myself on the narrow sidewalks in order to be sure not to touch them.

On historic streets, past centuries-old buildings I walk, going by the neglected doorways and broken basement windows encrusted with dust. I learn how to hold my breath when a whiff of musty, centuries-old air gushes out as I pass. I also practise jumping over puddles of urine on my way to work. But I am not annoyed. It all goes with Paris's natural, uninhibited character. By the same token, no one finds my shabby clothes strange, any more than the long white robe that walks by itself down the darkened boulevard. Which up close turns out to be an African priest.

I proceed on my way to work, pass the just-opening cafés where the waiters are rushing, already in uniform and with perfectly smoothed-down wet hair, opening doors and windows to let out the night's stale cigarette smoke to mingle with the morning's August air. They hurry to turn chairs over with seats down on the tabletops, then pour buckets of water under them and let it, and whatever goes with it, flow across the sidewalk and into the street. All that is done with swiftness for the soon-to-arrive café-loving Parisians, who routinely rush out of their crammed apartments to have breakfast out on the boulevards, which they think they own.

On my way home in the evening, as Paris begins to move into full swing, the boulevards undulate with a mixture of people of remarkable diversity, and each is free to interpret his own nationality, race, political adherence and fashion, wearing it openly in a personal way. And the whores. As soon as the light gets dim, they appear from nowhere in their outrageous business outfits. And at practically any corner, the street orators have audiences gathered around—curious people stopping to boo or applaud the speakers' vehemently delivered views.

The cafés come alive like beehives, transformed completely from their sleepy morning faces. Animated conversation and contagious laughter spill out onto the sidewalks. Only the waiters are from a different breed, sliding impassively between palm-sized tables, deadly sure of their territorial rights, wearing a learned professional expression. The order has to be prompt, in clear, short, routine words—the habitual boulevard-stroller's language. They don't bother to bring out patience for timid, faltering patrons. I am too shy to sit down for a hot chocolate. Usually, I indulge in a ten-franc piece of raw coconut from a street vendor's stand if I am hungry, or simply because I want to be part of the casual hubbub on the street, on my way home.

The Métro is as packed as it is in the mornings, if not more so. One has to position oneself the right way at the right moment on the platform for a chance to get in. One evening, as I

150

squeeze myself into one of its cars, I hear a man's high voice calling in Hungarian to his apparently lost friend in the crowd: "Hol vagy Ödön?" (Where are you, Ödön?) The answer comes shouting from the open door area. "Itt vagyok, hát nem látod hogy a fél seggem még kint lóg?" (Here I am, but can't you see that half of my ass is still hanging outside?) Hungarians always think that no one is around to understand them. I wish at that moment that Hanna were with me so we could howl with laughter together.

I try to describe in letters to her what I experience and what I see. My words flow with unrestrained ease on paper, because, in my mind, we have never parted. It is as if we walked every step together, sharing it all. As if we admired the beauty around us, with her eyes and mine. Meeting some problem, we discuss it, then put it in its place. And if something interesting presents itself, maybe with a bohemian hue, we enjoy that, too.

Thinking of Hanna one day, I take the Métro to the Gallerie Lafayette (department store) to purchase the most appropriate thing I can think of to send from France, a perfume called *Soir de Paris*. Maybe my gesture, which I can't really afford, is a way of boasting of how well-off I am, also some proof that leaving Hungary was right. Though in 1948, Communism in Hungary is perfectly palatable for an honest believer in the ideology.

A few weeks later I get a phone call: the man is a cousin of Hanna's, resident in Paris and recently back from visiting Hungary, and he wants to meet us. That is how one day, instead of going to rue Richer for a free meal, Nathan and I are invited for lunch to a restaurant on the rue d'Italie. It is our first decent meal in as long as we can remember. It is also a first brush with normal life, with the way the majority of the world lives. Further, it fortifies my assurance that Hanna and I can reach out to each other, that we are not terribly far. He also surprises me by handing over an envelope from her with 6,000 francs in it, my salary for a week.

———

In the meantime, summer in Paris turns into fall, long and beautiful, then cold and rainy. And our hotel room turns from sweltering hot to icy cold. Maybe it feels even colder because of our growing uncertainty about when our stay in Paris will end. Then, in the middle of November, the JOINT abruptly decides, from one day to the next, to move us out of Paris. We get no information about the trip, but as so many times before, we go.

We have an eventful ride to the station; it happens to be the chaotic day of a general strike, which includes taxis. It becomes apparent when we meet our transport that our train is heading for Switzerland. Delighted, our group, people in transit like us, settle into the luxuriously upholstered compartments, into the immaculately kept, wine-red plush seats. There are nowhere hints of the unrepaired damage of war; I slide unnoticed into its peacetime atmosphere. The evidence of prosperity and well-being is topped only by the Swiss conductor's charm while inspecting our tickets. It is like watching a lighthearted musical. A tall, blond man (a Nelson Eddie) swivels around, collecting papers with an unburdened smile, like a gracious host with his favoured guests. While I follow his joyful, animated dealings with my eyes, I realize how much lightheartedness has faded from my life.

We land in a small but wonderful hotel: neat room, crisp bed linen, all soothingly orderly, in contrast with everything over the last five years. Nathan and I feel suddenly assured and comforted, even if only temporarily, by all the promising present. Being in the proper land of chocolates, under the influence of the moment, buoyantly, we allow ourselves a small bar of Suchard. Never tasted chocolate that good before. We spend a day in a world of peace. A single day, that is. A flashback to bygone years, where war neither penetrated nor left an aftermath, where values remained untouched, where soul-destroying cynicism couldn't get through.

But the next day, heaven ends. The entire transport loads onto buses, bound for Turin, Italy. Next, we find ourselves deposited in a huge vacant building, a former mental hospital, deserted and unprepared for any lodgers. The week drags on endlessly and we can't think of anything cheerful, not knowing how long our present state will last. We sit on top of our luggage, in the bare, austere, echoing stone corridor, staring out at the grey, damp days, waiting once more, blindly.

And then, as suddenly as before, we are back on the road. This time, from the bus window, we watch the road and guess our goal. We become sure we are heading south from Turin, noticing the weather getting friendlier by the hour. At last we recognize the city of Genoa, the port from which people usually embark.

Nathan and I quickly make ourselves comfortable in the pleasantly furnished hotel room. I rush to the window and push the shutters open. What a relief from foggy Turin! Bright sunshine comes in, and a mirthful singing with it, as if underlining the view: the flowery backyards, the open back windows with the white bedding hanging out to air. Someone, contentedly doing household chores, happily sings an aria from an Italian opera. The whole scene, and the singing, hurls me back ten years in a whiff, to when I was last in Italy, in 1938. I stand there in a storm of feelings, unrealistically charmed, and wondering how to make the parts fit, when I am yanked back to reality by Nathan's voice coming from the corridor saying, "Magyaro? Magyaro? Kom, kom [sic]." (Though not properly pronounced or spelled, it means: Hungarian? Hungarian? Come, come.)

He enters the room and behind him comes a Hungarian woman in a typical peasant's Sunday clothes: the dark gathered skirt, a black satin-cloth apron around her waist, the dark long-sleeved fitted top, and a black *babushka* tied under her chin. She holds her hands in blessing fashion, murmuring, "Oh, my heart," in anticipation of meeting her saviour, someone who speaks her own Hungarian tongue.

At once, she begins to pour her story out to me. From what I peel out of its centre, she has left Hungary by train to make, for her, the inconceivable trip to her family in Argentina.

153

Because she doesn't know a single foreign word, she lost her luggage when the customs agent called the passengers for luggage information at the Austrian border. She first discovered the loss here in Italy. She has lost the great wicker trunk. In it she has packed everything precious that she feels a Hungarian might lack on the strange soil of Argentina. In her warmhearted simplicity, she has packed the smoked meats and the baked goods, as if she were making a trip a few kilometres away from her own home town. She has also put her entire wardrobe in it, and her money, hiding it all deep in the trunk. Now she stands in front of me with a small wicker basket on her arm, the equivalent for her of a handbag, hiding only an embroidered white linen handkerchief, which is all she has now.

Without delay, I leave Nathan behind and take to the streets of Genoa with her, where I myself am a first-time visitor. I am on the chase of the Hungarian consulate, hard to find after the war, as Hungary is seemingly not organized yet and hasn't decided about its own representatives. The search, as it turns out, is a full day's work. I crisscross the city by streetcar with her, with my minimal knowledge of Italian, until I manage to dig up some leftover diplomat acting as a representative, and leave her in his care. I undertake this effort without thinking of doing otherwise, inspired by my upbringing to stand by if encouragement or assistance is needed. Plus, I have my own sentiments for my country's rural values, which are still an intrinsic part of me. I have to comfort her, though I guess, rightly, the woman is about to meet her family, who escaped at the end of the Hitler era to Argentina. But I feel as if my father has led me by his spirit: forgiving weaknesses without embarrassing.

———

After two nights in Genoa, we start a chaotic embarkation on an Italian ex-military boat, the *Leme*, worn to its ultimate puff and on its last voyage. We go onward with our luggage in one hand and our boarding passes in the other. All the passengers carry them, with bed or bunk numbers on them, and we advance excruciatingly slowly. Nathan and I lug and haul our suitcases side by side, until at one point we are separated as we are told that men and women travel in different compartments. I go down the stairs, more and more sets of stairs, deeper down into the boat's belly, until there are no more stairs.

I find myself part of a milling group of at least 150 Italian women. Astonished at the huge, walled-in place, I seek a spot to rest a moment with my load. I check my boarding pass for my bed number and begin to circle around the bunk beds. I circle and circle again and once more around, then again in hope of finding my nonexistent number. That fact takes me a while to realize; I ask myself in disbelief, "Why me?" Then I push my luggage somewhere out of the way while I search for a crew member for help. But the confusion still goes on, and I find the crew as overwhelmed as the nervous crowd. Finally, I give up. I can't see myself discovering by chance a bed or even a chair to call my own for the next few weeks.

Just then I feel a movement, and hear the sharp steamy whistle. Leaving my possessions carelessly behind, I run upstairs to the deck to witness the moment when we glide away from the shores of Europe. I want to remember forever the slowly disappearing landscape and my fading old continent. Alone on deck, doubt and uncertainty overcome me, as I stand between my memories and nothing. And then, even the memories I have are only half there, because I hold away those that I can't allow myself to believe are my own.

Aftermath

It is now 1994, almost fifty years from the day I was abruptly removed from my established habitat, ripped away from my loved ones, stripped of everything that made up my life, dumped like trash into a forsaken place to find myself in the fire of purgatory, and left with nothing but naked existence: a life that didn't seem worth the effort of living. My memories, the images of the life I had known, froze into a solid block, forming a wall that separated me from the inexplicable present.

When the miraculous moment of freedom arrived, it was not the way I expected it. It was not as I had hoped to find it at the end of a long, vacant path. Life didn't wait to be continued as if it had not been interrupted. Freedom arrived, but it was an empty freedom, holding no substance. There was no link left back to life.

The world, relieved of the pressure of war, made a frightening discovery: we were still alive, though it could deal with the painful reality only in one big lump. To make it simple, to understand who we were, we became known as Displaced Persons—for short, D.P.s. In the public eye, under that catch-all name we all represented the same image—those who had escaped the same fate. We alone knew that those of us who came out were not identical. But the times did not care about individual hurts. We were too many, so we were fused together. There was no time to mourn. There was only time for the necessities, the day-to-day struggle of surviving our freedom.

So it was that I heaped layers and layers of years over the repressed memories; and the years just went on.

My search for freedom continued, first through Ecuador for fourteen years. There, the strangeness of the land with its disastrous natural elements, its culture, its frightening mixture of the pagan and the Christian, the learning of a new language, and the striving for mere subsistence allowed no repose. Particularly difficult years went by for me, years filled with disappointments as my vain attempts to have children overshadowed everything else. That sad fact became a painful complex of failure for me—my own failure, I thought. Nathan didn't find it significant. Another break and a new start became inevitable.

Then, a few years later, when I had sadly given up hope, my two sons were born—like a gift—into a new marriage. From then on, my family was my sole interest, as I knew I had reached as close to a full life as I could ever envision. At last, I attained the harmony of a family life. I dedicated myself gladly to the most important task of all. I also guarded my past carefully from my children, hoping to convey a positive outlook and not to let hate enter and distort their view of life.

From Ecuador, our search led us to Australia. The boys were hardly four and six then. But I could not settle there either. Though I learned my fourth language and tried to fit in with the character of the country, to bend myself to its terrain, I never felt part of it. I tried to meet Australians, but kept my experiences quietly inside, afraid I would distance people or scare them away. I wanted desperately to be just like everyone else around me. This effort resulted in my living only on the surface, and, after six years, we left.

Then, twenty-three years after my physical liberation, due to my husband Henry's wise decision, good luck led us to

Canada. We still think about the momentous event of our arrival with gratitude.

I will feel forever thankful to Toronto, to Ontario, to Canada, but first and foremost to all the "WASPs" who laid the foundations to create this city. I am thankful for their stable culture and their principles, for their unconfusing, solid outlook, for their puritan, rational traditions. Their sense of security and strength allowed me time to relax, to ease my way into the country's true nature, and to feel as close to being "at home" as I could hope to be.

———

In 1969, I made my first trip back to Hungary. I thought the country was like a sinister monster; a dust-covered steel body with cold, staring eyes and sharp steel teeth, biting without mercy for survival.

I found very little of the Hungary I knew before, hardly anything charming, and very little that was moving. For short moments I could rejoice at seeing a Hungarian plant, or fruit, or the sweet taste of a middle-European breeze. But I couldn't speak, and even to mention dear, lost names would sound like blasphemy to me. The atmosphere did not lend itself to remembering. I also sensed that people interpreted the same memories differently. It wasn't possible for me to share the twenty-five years I had lived apart from them either till then. It would have been out of place there to speak about my struggles, my longing, my homesickness. As a result, I left for Toronto empty-handed from my first visit back to Hungary.

I wanted to search for my past, but feared to find it. However, Hungary attracted me again and again, like a magnet. Though I was unable to communicate with my relatives, they were endlessly patient with my silence and accepted what I had become, based on their memories of me from before. And for me, every meeting was like a booster that gradually helped me

159

to reconstruct my identity. I kept returning for portions of reassurance, for their way of talking, for the sound of idiosyncratic family words and phrases, for a dose of reality—a lost reality. My emerging relaxation, incidentally, almost paralleled the relaxing of Communism's hold on Hungary.

On my fifth visit back in 1987, my cousin Ivan made a surprise stop with me—at my birthplace. Then, in his unintrusive, considerate, sensitive company, I was able to let the memories come back to me with less fear.

My visit broke open the crust that had been closed for forty-three years. Not that I lived the years before this moment without being aware of the past at all—but I only recalled the pleasant memories when I needed assurance of purpose in life to go on while part of the past lived its own hidden, petrified existence. "The Visit" was the result. It took an additional nine years to put the painful, jagged words, one by one, on paper, to complete the full cycle. My visit released me into an elating new freedom, simultaneously awakening my strong desire to share the spirit of the past, its slow pace, a gradually fading way of life.

The Visit—My Other Self

On one of the last days of April 1987, I make another visit
to loved and shunned memories. My cousin Ivan is driving me to Budapest from Dunajska-Streda, which used to be in
Hungary before the war but is now in Czechoslovakia. It feels
simultaneously familiar and unreal to be here; it is the way I
feel every time I come back.

We ride on delightfully quiet roads in his small car, "made
in Czechoslovakia," where privately owned vehicles are luxuries. In it, we sit low (unusually so, for me), close to the
ground. The reluctant, noisy motor quivers through to the
seats. The car is not built for comfort; it has hardly any shock-
absorbing springs.

We drive on the sun- and shade-streaked road under the
poplars. The horizon is unlimited here on flat land, in the
Middle Danube region. The view of the pastureland and farmland is wide open on both sides. Fresh crops—sown well ahead
in the fall—stick out already, forming an even, fresh green car-
pet; it adds to the promising, cheerful, quiet scene. Through
the open window, my hair is blown by the light breeze; it keeps
me in direct touch with the seasonal weather and the outside
world. The view can release rapture and soothe at the same
time. It is spring.

Our car is like an unfit disturbance—the only one in sight—in a harmonious picture. I have a strong desire to freeze the present moment and never let it change, though I also know the country's hope is prosperity and progress via modern technology. It may be hard to change peasants' traditions, and I hope they don't let it happen too fast.

I try to carry on an intelligent conversation and, at the same time, express my thanks through my attitude, since Ivan came from Budapest especially to meet me and take me back.

I look eagerly to my right, to my left, so as not to miss anything. I want to suck in all the pictures, hold them, store them deep and take them with me past oceans and skyscrapers to my faraway world.

The mood of my day-and-a-half-long visit in Dunajska-Streda with my late father's last living cousin, Nora, still travels with me.

I come here from time to time from a different life, to find repose with her in the unchanged tempo of bygone times, to strengthen myself and reset my life's clock again by the past's mirrored reflection.

Nora is eighty-three now. She lives in a tiny apartment in Communist Czechoslovakia, all alone. I always arrive unexpectedly, and at every visit find in her the serenity of a nearly forgotten world. She accepts whatever life brings with calmness, grown from roots in the past.

She serves her meals on the small kitchen table, which she pulls out into the middle of the kitchen; her meals are like festive banquets. When she invites me to sit down she has a modest, but proud knowing smile on her face. I smile too. She knows well that I notice and appreciate her crisp damask tablecloth and the subtle respect and care with which she puts the food on it. And we both know what the other is thinking. Our kinship allows us to share the feeling, and the thought. The colour of our looking glass is reassuringly the same.

Now, watching the road, I am caught between three worlds: the past, the present, and the present back home. I try to hide behind conversation but find myself entangled in uncertainty.

"Sorry Ivan, Nora doesn't know I asked you for a ride. She thinks you acted behind her back by taking me away. I couldn't tell her before you arrived that I was leaving."

"I hope," Ivan replies, "she'll forgive me when I come to see her again in two weeks."

His answer makes me feel better, but the fact that I don't know this person beside me, my cousin Ivan, keeps me slightly on edge, though we have met every time I have visited Hungary since the war. He is a charmer, a very likeable fellow, but I know only as much about him as he wants me to know. I am the one who holds the connecting thread between us, though not insistently; I make it only as binding and as personal as I suppose he can accept.

He is one of the few people left from my family, he is part of a mutual line, and an important link to that constant companion in my life: the past.

Aunt Flora, his grandmother, and Katica, my grandmother, were sisters. Both are dead now. But only Katica was given the right to go with dignity. Flora was not blessed with a civilized death.

I wonder what he thinks about me, what he can see of me through my actions, what he surmises through gossip, good or bad, what he can see of my years on the other side of the globe. He never asks anything; he never tells me anything.

So we talk about someone else; that feels more comfortable, though we are still not fully at ease.

Meanwhile I keep my eye on the road. It is spring in Czechoslovakia, the warm, promising, crystal-clear spring I remember. It enters cautiously, delicately; the kind of spring found only in Europe.

163

The morning has only started; a woman looks approvingly along the finished rows in her vegetable garden while she tightens the knot in her red babushka with muddy hands. Then she bends over again to put more onion bulbs—saved from last year's crop—into the moist soil, one by one.

Tiny, whitewashed, thatch-roofed village houses show through weather-beaten wooden fences as we drive by. The yards are active, just as they used to be in springtime. All the birds, animals, pigeons and other creatures whirl about each other, regardless of species or origin, united in cacophony for their morning feed. Newborn chickens follow the hen's protective call, running. Everything bustles with the tempo of the season, trusting the continuous rhythm of the years.

Soon we arrive at the sobering reality of the Czech-Hungarian border, where passport checking is a serious business. We are ordered out of the car and hand over the passports. Ivan, being familiar with the procedure and the time we will waste, suggests settling down for the long wait. "Do you want a coffee?" he asks.

"Sure, why not."

He brings it over. We sink with it into the broken springs of the worn, dusty sofas in the waiting corner. The espresso tastes poisonous; it is shockingly strong. But everybody drinks it eagerly and incessantly. This is still a surprise to me on my visits. I remember when espresso was a leisured people's drink in these countries.

It seems to be accepted now, a legitimate break from work. At all times, everybody reaches for the cup routinely and as often as possible, wearing a uniformly serious countenance and making believe that it is an important part of the job—a cunning, wordless sabotage, a convenient valve to let out the boredom and the anger people dare not express.

Before, espresso drinking was a harmless little pleasure. The quiet, respectful atmosphere, the subdued, polite waitress in a black silk dress with a white Swiss-batiste apron is not around here anymore. Now the coffee clatters across the counter in a chipped cup, spilled on the saucer carelessly. It has become commonplace, and that has taken away its subtle charm.

While we sip our coffee and Ivan draws on one of his numberless cigarettes, we talk about my visit with Nora, about her son Peter, who is divorced now but spends all his free time with his ex-wife and his children. Ivan mentions how unpredictable Peter is, even with his mother. But I make excuses for Peter, mentioning his difficult position with Nora. She relies on his help daily in all her out-of-house matters, disregarding his personal life. She expects him to be at her service but doesn't appreciate his efforts. With her good Austro-Hungarian upbringing, giving orders come naturally. Peter is fifty-one now.

Ivan listens, agrees half-heartedly, indifferently, making no effort to go further into the matter. I look at him across the table. He appears broken and tired for his age. His nicotine-yellowed fingers, his carelessly chosen clothes, reveal his disillusionment.

I would like to talk to him about it, to express my sympathy, though it would be futile, I know. His detached solitary nature, together with his fatalistic outlook, usually allow only a polite, noncommittal, "You think so," followed by a friendly, cough-like laugh.

Recalling him in his youth and piecing it together with the present, I think that fatalistic streak was always there in him. Perhaps through the years it penetrated deeper.

He lost much on account of the war, but he is as silent about that as about everything else. His outstanding marks at the Benedictine grammar school led him nowhere. The numerous *clausus*, which restricted the number of Jewish students at universities, made it impossible for him to study further. Then came the "Jewish Law," which left only manual work open to Jewish youth in Hungary. As a last choice he took up horticulture; he may have had the family estate in mind for later. But after the German occupation it was taken over by the Communists. I lost track of him during the occupation and in the years after that. Now he is married and has a beautiful daughter, Dolly. That was the name of his sister, lost in the war. Dolly is deaf and mute.

As far as I know, he suffered many hardships under the Communists. At last, he is in a position where he can put some of his artistic talents to use. Who knows what happiness means to him, but he doesn't seem really happy now, in spite of his constant joking. Maybe his passive, torpid resignation is best summed up in his own self-amusing words: "I believe Communism is still better than working."

The customs officer at last appears with my passport, but for some sinister reason he won't hand it over before I pay an extra $40 US. Of course it cannot be in Czech korona, which I was forced to buy upon entering the country.

Yet another procedure is still to come: the baggage inspection. "Did you buy anything in Czechoslovakia?"

"What can you buy here?" I answer. That honest joke nearly turns into a disaster.

He fixes his intimidating eyes on me for a few alarming moments and barks: "What, what are you saying? Are you offending my country?!"

I reply as if it is an afterthought, and still keep my smile, "I have everything, I don't need anything."

"Just be careful," he snaps, and after a long tense silence and menacing look, he lets me go.

I feel stupid. What a blunder. Ivan is speechless. He was not sure what the outcome of that annoying incident would be, I can see. My excuse is weak, that I couldn't imagine that such hot-headed patriots still existed in the Eastern bloc. Maybe I have become too secure and overconfident, as though freedom of speech were guaranteed forever.

Relieved, we take to the road again, driving through Komarom. This is another town I am attached to, another town to grieve. My grandmother's youngest sister, Aunt Hermina, and her family lived here. I am searching eagerly for their house as we roll on. I glimpse it down in a side street.

Fragments of episodes of their lives, and of ours with them, weigh me down. They come strangely close; I feel disconnected in time. I see Aunt Hermina, content as always, radiating the joie de vivre that is characteristic of her. Her grown-up children, Sarika and Bandi, confident and proud; they are reflections of their mother. I see her during those strenuous years when she had to face her husband's blindness and early death. Then, in the times when she managed the family business alone, while smoothing and watching over Sarika's and Bandi's future. She was always in good spirits, never letting them know her anxieties, which she must have kept under the surface. All that she mastered with an inspiring élan; to others, it looked brilliantly easy.

Many years later, when I knew more of life, I asked her spontaneously, "Aunt Hermina, how do you manage to be always in a good mood?"

"Oh, my dear child," she said. "I am not always in such a good mood, but people don't like to see tears. I think tears should be hidden in laughter."

Her daughter Sarika was by far the best-dressed, best put-together young girl, later woman, that I knew. Her pleasing looks left one spilling over with contentment. Tall, slim, elegant and cool, she was as uplifting as a harmonious work of art.

Though Sarika had her own distinctive taste, Aunt Hermina played her own definite part in Sarika's creation, by forming her attitudes and bearing, not to mention the becoming background which she arranged as only a good impresario could.

Sarika married young—too young—to a perfectly mannered, astute businessman, Schiller Pali, who entered the family business. Aunt Hermina must have prompted Sarika's decision; she had managed the business until then.

A few years later, Zsuzsika was born. Pali engaged a nurse, Tesza, to be ready in her white uniform weeks ahead of the birth. And from her birth on, Zsuzsika was sheltered, cared for and jealously watched over by Tesza. Pali wanted to bring up an ideal baby—his ideal—and kept a close eye on her progress, as on everything else, whether family or business.

The stories about the measureless protection of Zsuzsika were told in the family with smiles. Not knowing what the future held, we laughed.

The last time I saw Sarika was on her holidays with her brother, Bandi, in the mountains near our place. Those were already the breath-holding times when all Europe burned in high flames around us. She dropped in for a visit, wearing her brown-chequered riding breeches and a sporty, shimmery-brown, short nutria fur. Her glossy black hair she wore—according to the fashion—in Cleopatra-style. I found her remote and aloof. Deliberately, I asked her questions to shock her into reality.

"What made you decide to have a child?"

She looked at me motionless for a while with her big clear eyes, and then, "I thought I'd try that too," she said.

Uncomprehending, I regarded the answer as haughty and evasive. Now, too late, I understand the truth. "The beautiful woman" was the only role left for her amid mother, house-keeper, nurse, businessman husband. And it was not enough.

When the Germans overran Hungary, Zsuzsika was sent into hiding with Tesza. She was about four then. The parents sailed to Palestine on a rented boat that never arrived.

Bandi had the same God-given good looks as his sister; but he was more outgoing, quicker to laughter. He never said "no" to fun. Women adored and spoiled him.

I can never forget him in his riding suits, or in his Czecho-slovakian artillery officer's uniform, or dancing a *csardas*, or just giving me, en passant, a loving little pinch on my cheek and saying, "What's doing, little girl?" But not with an adult's condescending attitude; rather it was an appreciative, encouraging gesture.

He wasn't a guest in our house. He came and left as he pleased, as if ours were his second home. We were all pleased to have him around. And he always was around. His very being was woven into my childhood and adolescence.

Bandi loved life and lived as if life were there to enjoy. His looks, his gregariousness, supported his right to it. He assured me from time to time: "As soon as you turn eighteen I'll take you out to The Kioszk."

That future event, I believed then, would be my initiation into real life. The Kioszk was on an island in the middle of the city. For a young girl, being invited to The Kioszk meant being appreciated. It also meant sitting on a warm summer night upon the glittering open terrace where waiters in tuxedos slid between tables quietly while the orchestra played soft music. And when the music paused, the guests' high-pitched laughter echoed through the river, to the other side where the willows bent in the warm night breeze.

Circumstances changed; he never took me there.

For forty years, I evaded examining my thoughts or coming to conclusions about Bandi, but now I feel ready. I also recognize my chance, riding now with Ivan alone. I take a deep breath.

"You must know more than I do, you hid in Hungary like Bandi during the German occupation. Do you know what happened to Bandi?"

"You must have heard," Ivan begins. "He joined an underground counter-revolutionary unit under Lieutenant Gidofalvy. He wore a Hungarian officer's uniform; he also changed his name. He was quite a guy, if you remember him. It wasn't his style to give his life away without resisting. His unit sabotaged whatever was possible and saved whom they could under those ghastly conditions. He managed to save his mother's life."

We drive silently for awhile. I watch the passing scenery interlocked with sceneries in my mind; our life before and now.

The catastrophic drama took place here on the same soil under my feet. Does anyone stop life here for a moment to remember, to ask: "Where did those people go?" Does anyone remember Bandi? Why, he thought the world belonged to him: the sidewalks where he walked, the houses he passed, the trees, the bank of the Danube. Is there a vacant, unfilled gap now? Nobody remembers, nobody thinks that the fresh, new leaves and the bright spring sunshine are cruelly sad; only me.

Everybody rushes about their daily chores, unconcerned; walking, chatting, continuing life's unmistakable order, as we did then—until the friendly spring sunshine ended in the diabolic annihilation of all sunshine, all springs.

Ivan goes on: "He was arrested by the Gestapo, but somehow he forced open the cattlecar floor and jumped off the moving train—would you believe it—at Komarom."

I see him clearly in front of me. I see his vigorous, resolute movements. The risk he took goes through me. I can see him rolling down the railway embankment. Did he choose a grassy spot? A deep marshy one, with tall rushes? Was it close to the Danube? Did he feel more confident because it was his home town? What were his thoughts then?

I have to interrupt Ivan to change the topic.

"And I have also never heard what happened to Zsuzsika during the war."

After considering where to start, he says, "Bandi got false papers for Zsuzsika, too. Later, when Budapest became too dangerous, Tesza took her to her own home town as her illegitimate child."

"Wasn't Tesza single?"

"Oh, she went beyond loyalty, though after the war was over she didn't find the peace she deserved, either. Zsuzsika's uncle (her father's brother) came back, and claimed the child, and took Tesza to court because she refused him. Her argument was: 'Zsuzsika must stay with me; I promised Mr. Schiller that

I wouldn't entrust her to anybody unless her parents came to take her.'"

"She lost. The court appointed the uncle as her guardian. But later, he put her into an orphanage. It took years for Aunt Hermina to get her back, and by then Zsuzsika was already sixteen, and Tesza had died."

"This isn't a happy story either, Ivan. But at least Aunt Hermina was around her when she married and had her family." The boys were about ten when I first visited them. It was on my second trip back to Hungary, when I could afford it at last. Aunt Hermina got a lift for her and me in a car, in her magical way; cars were not everyday means of transportation.

During our drive, I listened to her account of "Zsuzsika-meets-future-husband." The story wasn't new, but she loved to tell it. She turned toward me, putting her hand on my arm. "And I also brought many other young couples together. I have to admit, I got an incredible kick out of it." Her whole face lit up, remembering it.

Now I regret deeply that I didn't realize why she arranged that visit. It only came to me much later. She hoped that eventually I'd take some responsibility for her adored granddaughter in Czechoslovakia. It was and still is hard to make ends meet there.

"I think, Ivan, a year after that visit, Aunt Hermina died? But she wasn't actually sick, was she?"

"No, she was not. She simply went into hospital, and from then on she refused food."

"My God, Ivan, she mentioned something like that last time I saw her! 'If I knew when I was going to die, I would pack my suitcase in order to spare my Zsuzsika the trouble.'"

"And she was strong enough to keep to her plan," Ivan tells me. "'You don't have to visit me that often,' she said to Zsuzsika, 'I am fine here, you have plenty with your family and household.' Two days later the hospital called to tell Zsuzsika that she had died."

171

"She was an unbelievable woman, Ivan. Besides loathing the thought that she might eventually become a burden, she was able to hold on to her masterly face-saving ways throughout her entire life, even beyond her death."

It takes a while before Ivan decides to continue. "The last we heard of Bandi was just the day before the Russians freed Budapest from the Germans. His barracks were surrounded by the Hungarian Nazis, who demanded he be turned over. He managed to escape from the barracks. Supposedly, he and a few others were on their way to meet the advancing Russians, when they clashed with remnants of a retreating German unit. And that was all we knew."

"What are you saying Ivan, that was the last? You mean to say he died there?"

"Yes, on the last day of the siege."

"But it was not even certain he died. Maybe his wounds weren't fatal. Maybe he was just abandoned, left alone?"

"What do you think? I was in Budapest then. Who knows about anybody? Who could possibly know where anybody was? On that last day of chaos, you were lucky to escape with your skin."

Ivan offers a poor consolation: "He was remembered later, at an official commemoration, together with other resistance fighters. His mother was invited. There is a street named after him: Szonyi Szucs Andras. Somewhere in Budapest."

Is that unchangeable then? The end?

Or could we try it once more? When we understand it better?

If only I could forget the past and live life without it; but I can't live without the past for the sake of those Hungarian Jews who were devoted Hungarians and now are lost, for the sake of those who survived, bearing the profound scar of a betrayal, and still remained loyal, and for the sake of a world that is gone forever.

The trees pass wordlessly.

———

"Ivan, Ivan," I shout in a flurry, "do I know this railway crossing here?"

He says nothing. Well, I say to myself, a sense of direction was never my strong point. I keep watching the road, comparing my feelings about Canadian and Hungarian landscapes. There is no doubt, this soil is close to me in spite of the pain. Its atmosphere, its familiar vegetation, its Hungarian road signs. I read all of them as we pass by.

Suddenly I spell out: "'Szent Pál Puszta.' Ivan, where are we going?"

"At last you recognize it, I was just waiting for it to sink in."

Szent Pál Puszta was a farm not far from Győrszemere (Szemere), the place I was born. Whenever the farm's nameplate came in sight on the way from Győr, I knew that home was close. Now I can hardly believe my senses.

"Why didn't you tell me we were on our way here?"

"I don't know. I just thought of it on the road. Anyway, I only came for you." And with a sideways smile he adds, "To tell you the truth, I never come here. It doesn't interest me at all."

I can't understand him. He grew up here too. The whole family was devoted to Szemere, it was home for us all. Every one of us came back here, to relax, to cry, to complain, to confess, to take new courage. Has he forgotten all that? Or there are other reasons I don't know?

True, I was not his friend. Rather my brother, Miki, was his companion in vacation-time and on weekends when he came to town to stay with his grandmother. And that was often. It seems he was always there. He was closer to me in age, but I was a girl.

Those two roamed about, nobody knew where, unless smoke was seen coming out of a haystack, or Ivan began to run around all in a fright with his new pants torn because Miki had used a vine-prop to help push him up a tree. Or unless I got a glimpse of them vanishing with the wooden wash-trough on

173

their heads in the direction of the swollen river with kayaking ideas. Their contriving was interrupted only by the midday church bell, which meant lunch time. To miss it was equal to a criminal act. Then, my brother would arrive panting, sticky-faced, worriedly trying to beat the steaming soup tureen to the table. For the rest of the day, nobody asked where they were. I did not have the same freedom; my steps were measured out for me.

Now we are driving on a road I thought had long ago fallen into oblivion. Seeing it brings back the past as if it were yesterday.

We pass the forest, which hides the small railway station. I knew that station as I know the palm of my hand. For seven years, the steam engine came puffing in every morning at 6:30 to take me to school in Győr.

If I was a few minutes early, I had time to take out the bag my mother had sewn for me, untie its string and pour out the treasury of buttons on the waiting-room table for a fast game of shooting buttons. Then someone—whoever heard the roaring—would shout, "The train!" and I would pack the buttons as fast as I could and manage to be outside when the engine reached the station, belching, sneezing the warm steam up on my feet.

All the children on the train—in the designated student car—were from neighbouring towns. They were the children of the farmers, the teachers, the postmasters, and sometimes even of poor labourers whose greatest dream was to have an educated descendant. From their lunchboxes came the enviable aroma of smoked *speck* between slices of black peasant bread. At 2:00 in the afternoon, we boarded the train for the trip back. They nibbled on the leftovers, the smell the more tantalizing before my lunch at home.

We are close to the bridge now where the Bakony-ér runs underneath. Not much of a river, but the only river we had. And the kind of fun we had there, that anyone could wish for on a hot summer's day. Plenty of leeches were in it too, but they were only a threat to those who stood still. Jumping and swimming were no problem for me. And if a leech did stick to your leg, the boys would hold a burning match to its tail and it would fall off in no time.

We got into the water in our rough country way, which was scorned by the city kids; perhaps their disdain was just a clever disguise for their lack of skill. We would sit down on the muddy, slippery bank and slide through the reeds and river plants into the cold water. Splash.

The surrounding pasture came right down to the river; it was full of sweet-smelling, bright yellow meadow-saffrons, saturated with water to a silky tenderness. Seduced by their shining yellow, and picturing them in my own vase, I often picked the easily broken stems, only to realize, holding a bunch in my arms, that they had become lifeless a few steps away from their wet soil.

After a few hours of ceaseless water games, we would lie down in the fresh grass, happily exhausted, the chamomiles, daisies, poppies, cornflowers around us. Also the bees and the flies. Even a bored cow might satisfy her exploratory stroll by snuffling, blowing hot air onto our unsuspecting bodies. If we looked back, we found ourselves in a close tête-a-tête with a pair of huge nostrils.

The mayflies dared to come out only later in the afternoon in a frisky chase over the water, their bluish, translucent wings nearly brushing it, when the sun's rays were no longer direct. We watched their chase and felt its light-heartedness while getting ready for home.

Down the river, close to the town, was the water-driven flour mill, where our goose-girl used to take the geese or ducks to feed on the pasture. Once, when I was about five, my mother let me go with her when she took a bunch of ducklings.

We shuffled after our charges in the dry mid-summer heat on the rutted, dusty road, they soundlessly and we sleepily across the bridge, where there was not a speck of shade. It seemed to take forever to get them across and I began to doubt the fun in my outing.

But as soon as the ducklings caught sight of the pasture, they revived; they opened their short, fuzzy wings to help speed their brand new yellow feet, uttering prompting murmurs to each other. It looked at first as if we had lost them, for they went crazy on seeing the tender grass ahead. In a moment they settled, though, devouring it as if they had never eaten before.

Soon their stomachs were full, bulging all the way to their necks. Then one by one they sat down, with inherited wisdom, under a shady tree in satisfied silence. And that should have been the sign to push homeward again, but we decided to give them a little more time to digest.

Later, laziness inspired practicality. "Mariska," I said, "why don't we send them into the river and let them swim over? so we could walk across the bridge faster."

She found it a good idea, and so we did. Gesturing widely with our arms, we got the resting flock reluctantly to their feet, and shoved them down to the river bed. A few took the hint at once, gliding into the water, and the rest followed the daring.

We speedily ran across the bridge to the opposite shore to welcome them from their very first dip into water. And soon the puffing, fighting ducklings appeared, shaking their feathers off, coming out onto the safe shore.

Unfortunately they didn't all come. Some couldn't make it. They were caught by the current around the big wooden paddle-wheel beside the mill. We waited and waited amid duck-calls: calls for help from the mill, and answers from the shore.

At last there was no use waiting anymore. We left the crying ducks behind and plodded home after the rest, to let them waddle silently into the yard. A few days later some teenage boys heard the stragglers' calls while swimming and ventured to take out a few more.

Shortly after the river comes a grassy clearing, then a hillock where "The Old Cemetery" was—that's what we called it. It lay in the acacia grove. Rain or shine, I passed it daily on my early morning ride to the station. In May, when the acacia was in full bloom, the hanging white cascades were a sure sign of the approaching end of the school year. The air, pregnant with the overpowering scent, slipped into my room through the open window, moist from the early dew, making me rise with a single jump.

A road led directly from the field behind our house to The Old Cemetery, which was a mystery to us children. Attracted and scared, we investigated closely the few weather-rubbed, mossy headstones, and peered one after another into the grass-overgrown crypt through the cracks in the dried-out doors. Then we ran away, shivering.

We arrive now and turn into "my" street at the corner where there used to be pasture land that belonged to us, but it is built up with houses. To my question about a recent decree, Ivan replies, "If nobody claims a property for a certain length of time, it goes back to the state."

And this is the corner where our dogs ran to meet us on the dot of three in the afternoon. They knew no limits the moment they spotted us coming. They broke out into a shrieking barking, and a skipping competition, colliding, then rolling on the ground, but never advancing farther. They stopped at the bridge. There, they jumped up to the horses, ran between the wheels, rushed a few yards ahead, then ran back to us again. At last, the triumphant time arrived when they could yap and bark us into the yard. While I was struggling down out of the chaise among them, I could hear my father's emerging voice, "Look at that, you'll get mud all over your coat, don't let the dogs jump on you."

We are now where our house is supposed to be. But it is not. It was an old-fashioned country house, built in an L-shape, with walls a foot-and-a-half thick. Along the inner side of the L ran a corridor with arches and columns, vaulted ceilings, the usual style in the country. The house would have been about two hundred years old now. For forty-three years, the old house had been unloved and uncared-for. I heard that it was stolen brick by brick.

Ivan stops the car. I don't get out. Through the window, my view glides from one point to another: the tall weeds, the remains of some garden flowers in between, the scattered, broken bricks. Far into the yard I notice, for no imaginable reason, that the well-bucket is still hanging on its pole, alone.

I can't speak. Such an inglorious end; I avert my eyes. I feel unreal. I feel as if I am falling into a timeless abyss. I see my parents, who lived as if they had their whole lives ahead of them; myself, as a daughter who believed this was a home to come back to forever; and as a mother who had hardly begun to be one. No trace, no sign, no sound, only me alone. Did my real life end then? Am I the same person who left with the parents, Raab Mihaly and Olga, and with my daughter, Hoffmann Katalin? This is not the me from then.

Ivan starts the motor. We pull away.

———

We drive farther down the road; passing the bare, abandoned, once-whitewashed, now-yellowed Catholic church; then Ivan's grandmother's house follows.

We don't feel like talking as Ivan slows down. I see the almost endless yard where cart-load after cart-load of fruit, hay or grains came in or out; the house lively under aunt Flora's strong hand; her married children; then, the grandchildren, who were taught here one by one (whose ever turn came) what a chamber pot was for. Or later, when the time came for high-school holidays, every grandchild rushed here happily. Now, only the walls stand, crumbling into decay.

Szemere appears empty and hollow as I look back at the street. A gray dust lies on it. It is without life. Not a soul on the street, or an animal or a cart. As it is so close to the city, a factory job is more advantageous. It doesn't pay to love the soil. It is like a manifestation of the cold, materialistic grip of Communism. Or perhaps of modern times?

As if it were yesterday, I see Aunt Flora's tall, erect figure advancing in the evening dusk, a faint smile on her face when she notices us outside, resting after a hot day. "Well, I nudged myself over finally," she would say, and sit down with slow majestic ceremony and a sigh, as if to say, Thank God, the day is over! After all that, she took her time, then looked around, acknowledging, resting her gaze attentively on everyone for a moment. Cousins, friends, neighbours, whoever happened to be there. Grandmother Katica was always there on her daily later-afternoon into later-evening visits. Flora was interested in everyone and everything. Familiar with everyone's affairs in detail, her questions circulated and her sound comments followed. Then she gave her own minute account of the day, which was what we were really waiting for.

Her smallest story had significance and was told with clear-headed intelligence; quietly, with short meaningful pauses in between, and sometimes a weak smile. Never a laugh, only a smile. She was a woman of integrity, but not cheerful. She lacked a light-hearted spontaneity. She was pleasant to be with, though sometimes embarrassingly realistic.

We lived quite close to each other, only five minutes apart on a child's running feet. My brother and I often moved like a pendulum between our house and Aunt Flora's, carrying messages, or a sample of something that had turned out especially well from my mother's oven. We were called in from wherever we were to rush it over, still hot—at its best. Or to return something she had borrowed from us, or we from her. Everything other than produce came from Győr.

The households in the neighbourhood or family circle were like an open book. Everyone knew the contents of everyone else's pantry. Menus were also discussed on those evenings together.

One afternoon when visitors dropped in, my mother called me and said, "Böske, set the table in the dining room." That day was a Monday. I knew that afternoon coffee also meant cake, which we had finished on Sunday. And Monday was not a day for cake-making either. I thought I hadn't heard right. But my mother reminded me again. So, I set the table. To my surprise, she put a beautifully iced pink rum torte in the middle.

Later I asked, "Where did you get that from?"

"Oh, Aunt Flora told me the other day that she had a rum torte sitting in the ice-pit. She got it from Zelma and doesn't know what to do with it. I sent the girl over to pick it up."

I saw Aunt Flora wearing her best only on a few special occasions. She never cared for a display in public, but her elegance even when she had on a simple housecoat came through. I remember her gray hair, loosely framing her face and forehead, kept together in a chignon on the neck. I remember her saying in the ghetto after her beautiful crown of hair was chopped off, "Böske, that will never grow back again."

I say nothing to Ivan. I can't share that memory with him.

Only a stone's throw away, on the opposite side of the street, lived Aunt Tera, Aunt Flora's sister-in-law. The two husbands were brothers. But as Aunt Flora married her uncle—her mother's brother—to keep family property together, her brother-in-law happened to be her uncle as well. I never saw the two women say a word to each other. Tera was an outsider: in Flora's eyes, "She did not fit in."

Tera was long-widowed, as Flora was. She had four children, married, or living away. She cared only about her children or grandchildren. Otherwise, she never had an honest conversation with anyone. She ran her estate cleverly, with calculating astuteness and unwavering thrift to the end.

I only went there when her grandchildren were around to play. On one such occasion she produced a snack that looked unusual to me; a slice of rye bread spread with buttermilk. I held it in my hand perplexed, until the dog, a white Bernandine, licked it off. When I held out the soggy, wet bread to her for help, she snapped, "You little rascal, you licked it off yourself, now eat it." It was my first encounter with an adult's false accusation.

She was out of bed at three every morning, when milking started. And she was about the whole day to keep an eye on whatever work was being done. Summer or winter, this went on until after dark. Then she went into her cold twilit kitchen—I happened to witness it once—shuffled around, tired, rubbing her cold hands together, looking for something pitiful to eat. None of her help stayed with her. She would grumble, and mumble to herself "These thieves, these bandits, would steal one's eye."

Tera lived a lonely life in her big house. Few people went to see her. It happened that as a teenager I sometimes accompanied my mother on her rare, dutiful visits. Then Aunt Tera used to complain in a weary, raspy voice, "You bad girl, you never come to see me." I never believed that her complaint was real.

A thin layer of used, wet straw was spread on the floor in the ghetto, to sit or sleep on. Otherwise nothing was in it, only the dirty bare walls. There she was, sitting on the floor with her aching body when the order came, "Move, hurry up, get going! You're going somewhere else." Everybody grabbed their own small bundle, the ultimate and last belongings, and rushed out—we didn't know then to where—leaving her behind, crying helplessly. My father, noticing that, took her heavy body with great effort on his back and carried her to the waiting train. We didn't know that the result would have been the same either way. She was together with Aunt Flora in the same cattle car that transported them to Auschwitz.

That all goes through me. While Ivan talks, my other thoughts continue and I am unable to tell them to him.

As we are close now, I ask him, "What's happened to your grandmother's vineyard?"

"It's all ploughed up," he replies.

Aunt Flora let us go there at any time. It was an outing for us children, an added freedom and privilege in our life. Only one warning reminder was repeated every time before we left: "Don't step on the raked sand." This frequent insider expression didn't need further explanation. We knew that it meant the sand about one metre wide in and outside the fence. The watchman raked it so as to recognize fruit-thieves' footprints. Otherwise, from spring to the end of the season we were free to come and go.

In the fall, grape-pickers carried baskets full of sticky, sweet-smelling grapes on their backs, followed and encircled by clouds of nervous, noisy bees. When the grapes were poured into the winepress, the bees, startled, changed the route of their chase to look for a new basket. I felt sorrow for the beautiful grapes' merciless end, but, like the others, I held my tin cup under the spout for fresh juice.

"We have to pass by your grandmother's house yet, and then the cemetery," Ivan proposes.

"All right, let's go there," I agree gladly. I wouldn't suggest he spend more of his time; after all, he said he was here only for me.

On our way, I spot my old stamping ground, the Calvinist elementary school where I was a pupil, and the adjacent church. In memory it was bigger, but on closer examination it is the same. And that takes me back through the years.

I see dear old Jakab, the parson, firm about my being at the church at seven every school-day morning. But our bond came from much earlier than my school years. He would come to our house, and I would sit on his knee and listen, staring into his bushy, black eyebrows, while he whispered stories in my ear.

He told them as if they were our secret. They were children's stories he had written himself. He also told me "Snow White" when I was sick with pneumonia and inflammation of the kidney at the age of four. I would have missed the play he directed, if he hadn't brought his cast of school children, all in costume, to my bedside before the show.

"What a good deed it is, Ivan, to bring me here. That was the best surprise ever." I know he can't imagine what it means to me, but I feel it deeply.

Generally, he keeps out of other people's business, and never does favours for anyone, so I wonder silently what his motive is now.

Still doubtingly, but with somewhat more trust, he accepts my praise. He becomes more talkative and asks me whether I remember this or that, what was on that corner before and what remains, and what else has changed.

"Here we have an espresso bar," he motions to the left as we turn.

"This is the last of all places I expected to see an espresso bar," I reply. "Where are the pubs? They used to be everywhere before."

I don't think he comprehends my wonder. He shrugs his shoulders; apparently he doesn't find anything strange about that. He grew into it gradually. For me, it is a fake Hungarian metamorphosis: city ways creeping into solid country life.

"Look up on the hill," he says." There's your grandmother's house."

"I can't see it. Where's the lower gate?"

"You see, where this new house stands," he explains. "At the foot of the hill, there was the lower gate. There are four houses in her yard, and there are two families living in her house."

I reflect on her character. Her memory in my mind is tranquil and untroubled. I know she is resting in peace in Szemere.

"I don't think, Ivan, you were ever with us when we were scrubbed and dressed to go visit my grandmother"—though I don't understand why. She came to our house every day. Anyway, we heard her voice calling the maid the moment she caught sight of us: "Come, my daughter, fast with the rag, wipe their shoes." We greeted her respectfully, with barely controlled vigour (good behaviour was hammered into us at home) and as tamely as we could, so as not to disturb the household peace. We followed her wordlessly inside and to the sofa, the usual place for children. In front of the sofa was a runner, not a real rug.

There on the sofa we sat, feet dangling in the air, looking straight ahead, in silence, so as not to look at each other and break into laughter. After what for us seemed an enormously long time, grandmother got up, heading toward the sideboard. We, knowing what was coming, sent elbow messages into our neighbour's ribs: her unforgettable cookies. I have tried to imitate these and many of her culinary arts through my life, and never could reach her heights.

A few impatient minutes after the cookies, we said, "We have to go home." As soon as we got through her door meekly, we broke loose to hop and run down the hill noisily, as fast as our feet could carry us.

At home, my father used to ask, "Tell me, what did your grandmother say to you?"

"Nothing," I would say.

"Nothing? absolutely nothing?"

"Nothing," I would say again.

"She didn't even say hello to you?"

"Yes, she said that."

Ivan stops the car and we get out on a secondary highway, in front of a patched-together wooden lathe fence.

"You remember Pista, the coachman? He always worked for someone in the family—my grandmother, your grandmother, or your father."

"Sure, I remember clearly that jocular fellow."

"He passed away suddenly not long ago. This is his son's house." He points behind the fence, down to the back of the yard to a modest, whitewashed dwelling. "Through his yard, you get to the graveyard," he says. "It's been squeezed in between peasants' properties."

Ivan opens the unlocked lathe-gate. The yard looks arid and lifeless, but at the gate's first squeak, from nowhere, a fox terrier—a scrappy little dog—runs at us with ear-piercing barks. I see, relieved, as I look to the house for help, that Pista's son is wandering out, followed by his teenaged daughter. He comes closer, with some distrust in his steps, until he realizes that one of the visitors is Ivan. The barking stops but its sharp sound keeps ringing in my ears. This is also the first "living" house I enter in Szemere.

In no time, maybe alarmed by the dog, or to see who the strangers are, more people gather. They must be from the neighbourhood nearby. Ivan tells them who I am: "Raab Böske," to make it clear. Raab Böske, my former name . . . the sound of repose, of anchor; Szemere, ancestral tunes; a moment's illusion. Tears are burning in my throat. In vain I try to swallow. They rush to the surface, like an avalanche.

I just stand there, embarrassed by my tears. I don't try to explain. Raab Böske stopped existing in their minds—maybe conveniently—a long time ago. I alone kept coming back in my thoughts, without laying claim to anybody's sentiment, atonement or repentance. But now, at the sound of my former name, the name of my youth, I realize that it is a longing for the sheltered feeling of my youth that has brought me back here. An illusion.

The last forty-three years roll in front of me in quick succession, as if unconnected with the here and now. As if it is me, but not me, standing here: the person who trod those alien roads through the years. Who became someone else. Who met a *world of strangers for whom I was born the moment we met,*

185

for whom I had no history, while for me, the past remained the true reality.

I stand here, torn. A part of me feels as if I never left, but the years of experience weigh on me: the disappointments overcome, the painful words of hostility and lies accepted and forgiven, the futile waiting for gentleness, for purity, for the genuine. I could only endure because I was once part of this place, the place where I learned to believe, to trust and to forgive. How can that be explained to these people? Can they trace that all back with me?

And now, is this the right place for my foolish weakness? Is this the right place to share my guarded pain? Where were these people—or anyone else in Szemere—when we needed help?

I can't block out my memories; I can't give up loving them. All I can do now is helplessly hold to my past, in reverence for my parents, for my father, who taught me only consideration, understanding; never vengeance.

Slowly, we move on to the small graveyard, where only members of our family are buried.

Leaving Ivan back in conversation, I go on by myself. Then I stop, stunned by the abandonment and neglect. There is no fence, no gate. The graveyard has become one with its surroundings: backyards, pigstalls, scratch-about chickens. I see a woman pulling away chunks of weeds, seemingly from my grandparents' grave. I call out to her, "How good of you." She doesn't know why I say so.

"Oh, these weeds grow all over my garden, I thought I'd clear them out," she replies, in explanation.

I realize she doesn't think about the graves underneath. Maybe she wasn't even born in Szemere. I can't expect her to care. I beg her to "clean that grave . . . keep it nice . . . maybe some flowers too?"

It appears that she understands me. I pay her. After she tells me her name, I remember her husband's family.

Ivan comes and joins me. "Let's go to the other cemetery," he says. On the other side of the road is the Christian graveyard. Everybody we have met till now follows us over.

It is a most tranquil place. All the graves are looked after. Flowers bloom on most of them.

I understand Ivan's reason as soon as I look at the names on the monuments. We both start to call out the names aloud, "Oh, you remember! Oh, my God!" And: "He died too!" Every name means an episode in our lives, and every episode comes alive. I am crying openly. I look at Ivan, who is shaking with grief. We can hardly go on. Still we walk slowly through the peaceful avenue of cypress trees.

I look down the hill into my grandmother's back garden. It is so close, I can see it perfectly. She could come out any minute with her parasol, in her black and white polka-dot dress, holding her small watering can, as she used to at this hour on springtime afternoons.

The air, the shadows, the sunshine filtered through the trees, the soothing breeze, the mildness of the late afternoon create the reposed, contented moment before nature steels to nightfall. Calm, motionless, like a painting by Botticelli, it holds me like a repetition of something, something I lived through once before. It allows me to be part of a soothing grief.

A woman is coming toward us under the trees, blinking her eyes and blinking again. Then she calls out in a flutter, "Ivan, Ivan, how nice to see you!" They hug, they cry, and then he asks her, "Do you recognize her?" pointing at me.

She looks, pulling back a bit, and then shouts, "Of course I recognize her, that's Böske. What a surprise. Oh God, and you know who I am? I am Treszka's granddaughter, you must remember her, she used to help at your grandmother's house. Oh, what a good lady she was. She fed us and she helped us without asking questions. And so did your father."

And then another woman, moving about the graves with plants in her hands, comes closer. "I went to Auschwitz," she says to me, "and looked up your father's name on the monument."

And I cry. I cry and cry.

Historical Notes to
And Peace Never Came

by Marlene Kadar

G yőrszemere, usually referred to as Szemere, is a village directly south of the large industrial city Győr, situated in the Transdanubian Kisalföld, or Little Plain. Elisabeth Raab fled her marital home in Pécs and returned to her parents in Szemere when the Germans invaded. She was vulnerable there. Just a few kilometres north of her in Győr was the German military headquarters for the area, one of ten in this particular collecting zone. This was Zone III; in total there were six zones in the Hungary of 1944.[1] One by one the Jewish inhabitants of each zone were visited by the SS (*Schutzstaffel*)[2] or its ally, the Hungarian gendarmerie; they were robbed, harassed, beaten and marched into makeshift ghettos—the Győr ghetto was created "according to an order from the Interior Ministry" on May 27, 1944—where they were humiliated and starved before they were "entrained"—sent off in cattle cars to concentration camps, mostly to Auschwitz/Birkenau. Yet even in the 1940s the 800,000 Jews of Hungary, unlike many other European Jews, were protected by the state until "it practically lost its independence."[3] The horrible tragedy of Zone III is that it, like other zones in the Hungarian-speaking regions, was annihilated rapidly on the eve of the allied victory.

Still a young woman in 1944, Elisabeth Raab was separated from her infant daughter and her parents overnight, never to see them again. It is a wretched fact that in Hungary all ghettoization and deportation plans were carried out as efficiently and quickly as they had been elsewhere in Nazi-dominated Europe, but in much less time. Because Hungary had been an oasis of safety for the first four-

and-a-half years of the war, Hungarian Jews believed that this catastrophe, too, would pass. The historian Randolph Braham reminds readers of the then oft-heard Hungarian phrase, *megússzuk*, "we'll get by."[4] Even Elisabeth thought she would get by; neither she nor her friends and family were fully aware of the atrocities of the Final Solution in Hungary and indeed elsewhere in Europe. How could they be?

The Uniqueness of the Hungarian Solution

Hungary adopted the first major anti-Jewish law in post-World War I Europe on September 22, 1920 (*Numerus Clausus* Act or Law XXV) under the leadership of the prime minister, Count Pál Teleki.[5] Under this law, a quota was placed on Jewish admissions to universities and other institutions of higher learning. The number of Jewish admissions was reduced to 6 percent; universities became hotbeds of anti-Semitism as non-Jewish intellectuals vied for the limited number of academic positions. Medical schools were particularly rampant with anti-Semitism; Randolph Braham explains that Jewish students were forced to use Jewish corpses for necrotomy, a practice that is forbidden under Orthodox Jewish law.[6] This law was short-lived, but it was the first to draw a distinction among Hungarian citizens on the basis of religious practices.

In spite of early signs of anti-Semitism, Hitler did not occupy Hungary until March 19, 1944, a date Elisabeth remembers well. Until that time, the majority of Jews in Hungary lived "a relatively normal life while the Jewish communities in the other parts of Nazi-dominated Europe were being systematically eliminated."[7] This makes the atrocities that Elisabeth Raab suffered all the more tragic. They could have so easily been prevented by those who did know what was going on in Europe. But no one came to her aid or the aid of her people. At the end of the book when she has gone back "home" Raab asks, "Where were these people—or anyone else in Szemere—when we needed help?" (p. 186).

As Irving Abella and Harold Troper so painstakingly document, "none is too many." Canada, too, could have helped. But Canada refused to rescue the Jews of Hungary from the onslaught that all nations in the West knew would befall them.[8] Not only did the leaders of the world know about the details of Auschwitz, but the victory of the allies was almost certain when Elisabeth, her family and her friends were taken away. We cannot forget that although Hungary was allied to the Axis, the right-wing government led by Miklós Kallay consistently rejected German demands for implementation of the Final Solution.[9] This means that when Hungary lost its de facto independence, it became a devoted accomplice to Hitler and to "the most ruthless and speediest extermination program of the Nazis."[10] As Daniel Jonah Goldhagen has recently attested,

> The last major national community of Jews that the Germans decimated was the Hungarian, a good portion of which they deported to Auschwitz in the summer of 1944. The war was clearly already lost, yet between May 15 and July 9 the Germans crammed 437,000 Hungarian Jews into 147 transports of scarce rolling stock, diverted from essential war activities. In the single most concentrated killing orgy at Auschwitz, the Germans immediately killed most of these Jews in the gas chambers.[11]

The Pre-War Anti-Jewish Laws

The First

Elisabeth Raab refers to the anti-Jewish laws on a number of occasions in *And Peace Never Came*. But for some readers, it is impossible to imagine what an "anti-Jewish law" would entail. Above I mentioned the first truly anti-Jewish measure, the short-lived *Numerus Clausus* of 1920. However, the spate of anti-Jewish measures and laws that prepared the ground for ghettoization, deportation and concentration in 1944 really got underway with *Law No. XV of 1938*. This law aimed to reduce to 20 percent the proportion of Jews in the professions and in financial, commercial and industrial enterprises where more than ten persons were employed. Until that target of 20 percent was achieved, Jews could not constitute more than 5 percent of the newly admitted. There were provisions for exemptions: for example, those who had converted to Christianity before August 1, 1919, and had maintained their affiliation with the adopted denomination uninterruptedly, were exempt.[12]

The Second

The radicals of the Hungarian right, spearheaded by members of the Hungarian Fascist party, the Arrow Cross party or *Nyilas* party, continued to pressure the government for further restrictions on the activity of the Jews of Hungary. They were generously supported by the Third Reich and a deepening anti-Semitic propaganda campaign. *Law No. IV of 1939,* "Concerning the Restriction of the Participation of the Jews in Public and Economic Life," assumed that not only were the Jews a threat to the economy and the culture, but they were alien and destructive, a separate racial group that did not easily fit in with humanity in general and with their host nations in particular. The second anti-Jewish law encouraged the government to promote emigration of the Jews. Hungarian Jews disputed the accusations: they attested their loyalty to the Hungarian flag. But as with the first law, the heads of the Christian churches supported the bill to its passing, even though many liberals and Social Democrats rejected it. It is interesting that many Christians did, however, criticize the racial aspects of the bill.

The 1939 act explicitly detailed what constitutes a "Jew," although the criteria are complex and are only summarized here.

The most racist articles of the law provided for the following policies:

1. Any person who himself belonged or one of whose parents or two of whose grandparents belonged to the Jewish community on or before the promulgation of the law was to be considered Jewish.
2. The law exempted those who were already Christians on the day of their birth or were baptized before their seventh birthday, and whose Jewish parent had converted before January 1, 1849.
3. Article 3 prohibited Jews from obtaining Hungarian citizenship either by naturalization or marriage.
4. It further prohibited them from holding any government position and provided for the retirement of all Jewish members of the court and prosecution staffs by January 1, 1940, and of all secondary and primary schoolteachers and public notaries by January 1, 1943.
5. It reinstated the 6 percent quota for admission of Jews to institutions of higher learning.
6. Licenses for the operation of a number of businesses were withdrawn and new licenses not issued until the 6 percent quota was achieved.
7. A firm with fewer than five employees could engage one Jew, and with nine employees, two Jews.

8. Jews were prevented from occupying editorial positions on the major newspapers and periodicals, and from producing and directing films and plays.[13]

It is clear that the second anti-Jewish law affected the entire Jewish community, but it had a particularly deleterious effect on two rather isolated groups: the 150,000 Jews in the territories acquired from Czechoslovakia, Jews who would have difficulty proving their Hungarian citizenship, and working-class Jews, salaried workers and unskilled workers alike,[14] whose power to determine the course of their lives was already limited.

The Third

The third anti-Jewish law, signed in August of 1941, declared "The Prohibition of Marriage between Jews and Non-Jews" and outlined harsh punishments for those committing violations. Based on the Nuremberg Law of 1935, it further narrowed the meaning of "Jew" to include, by implication, any person who had three or four Jewish grandparents, even if he/she was born a Christian. Moreover, marriage and extramarital relations between Jews and non-Jews were now completely outlawed.[15]

Historians believe that this, the most blatantly racist of the anti-Jewish laws, prepared the ground for the acceptance by the Hungarian peoples of the Final Solution implemented during the German occupation of Hungary in the final months of the war.[16] When Hitler finally overtook Hungary and its regent, Admiral Miklós Horthy, and installed the Hungarian fascist Ference Szalasi and the *Nyilas*, or "Arrow Cross Party, Hungarist Movement," so-called "ordinary Hungarians" were in a weakened state, ideologically prepared for "dejewification" by the three anti-Jewish laws.[17] The *Nyilas* coup produced *Nyilas* terror. Action followed ideology, and it followed swiftly.

The so-called "Hungarian Action" was overseen by Adolf Eichmann and the notorious Eichmann-*Sonderkommando* (Special command/department).[18] The Hungarian Action began on Elisabeth's mother's forty-ninth birthday, May 16, 1944, the morning when Elisabeth, her mother, her father and her two-year-old daughter "are taken for the last time out of [their] yard [in Szemere]" (p. 28). This is why peace never came. Raab writes: "[W]e are evicted, taken through the streets, out of the town. No one is out; or maybe they are simply behind the curtains. An epoch is closing. This is its end" (p. 28).

193

The End

For Raab it was not the end. At the moment when she was liberated, she had been "marching toward Bergen-Belsen, . . . the final point of our existence" (p. 59), the place she had imagined was the end. Although Raab was glad that *Deutschland [was] kaputt!* (p. 66), she realized that she had lost a part of herself. "An essential source, an affirmation of life, is gone," she writes, and she falls asleep a free woman, "without being able to grasp what freedom means" (p. 67). As Elisabeth respectfully observes toward the end of the book, "My visit broke open the crust that had been closed for forty-three years [and it took] an additional nine years to put the painful, jagged words . . . on paper" (p. 160). The first few years of the forty-three were terribly anguished, in spite of the obvious physical and mental relief the "freed" Elisabeth must have felt. It is at this time that she wanders across Europe, not knowing exactly who she is or where she belongs. She is a D.P., a Displaced Person, never fully able to resume her old life or former relationships, always feeling slightly at odds with everyone else and even with her own experience. As Elisabeth says early in the book: "I could not bring the inside and the outside close enough to meet. Ever" (p. 13). It is in this context that romantic and modernist investigations of identity and its frailty seem paltry. Homeless, rootless and worn, Elisabeth uses words and emotions sparingly to finish telling the story she must tell even though it does not bring the closure, the peace or the homeland she longs for.

With reluctance Elisabeth writes out the trauma of her life, but she never claims it fully for herself. It is, she warns in soft tones, the trauma of history, shared by many and suffered by others as good and as worthy as she. It is this modesty that makes Elisabeth Raab's life heroic and wise.

Notes

1 In 1944 the borders were increased to include Hungarian-speaking regions of Czechoslovakia and Ukraine. Raab refers to the city of Komarom, for example, a city which was then a part of Hungary, but which is now outside its borders.
2 The *Schutzstaffel*, literally the *defence echelon*, referred to the German police and security organization directed by Heinrich Himmler. See Ernst Klee, Willi Dressen and Volker Riess, *"Those Were the Days"*: The Holo-

caust through the Eyes of the Perpetrators and Bystanders, translated by Deborah Burnstone with a Foreword by Lord Dacre of Glanton (1988; London: Hamish Hamilton, 1991), p. 279.

3 Randolph L. Braham, "The Uniqueness of the Holocaust in Hungary," in *The Holocaust in Hungary Forty Years Later*, edited by Randolph L. Braham and Bela Vago, Social Science Monographs and Institute for Holocaust Studies of the Graduate School and University Center of the City University of New York (New York: Columbia University Press, 1985), p. 184.

4 Ibid., p. 190.

5 Randolph L. Braham, *The Politics of Genocide: The Holocaust in Hungary* (New York: Columbia University Press, 1981), Vol. 1, pp. 28-31.

6 Ibid., pp. 30-31.

7 Randolph L. Braham, "Preface," in *The Tragedy of Hungarian Jewry: Essays, Documents, Depositions*, edited by Randolph L. Braham, Social Science Monographs, Boulder and Institute for Holocaust Studies of the City University of New York (New York: Columbia University Press, 1986), p. vi.

8 Irving Abella and Harold Troper, *None Is Too Many: Canada and the Jews of Europe, 1933-1948* (Toronto: Lester and Orpen Denys, 1982), p. 180.

9 Braham, "Preface," p. vi.

10 Ibid.

11 Daniel Jonah Goldhagen, *Hitler's Willing Executioners: Ordinary Germans and the Holocaust* (New York: Alfred A. Knopf, 1996), p. 160. Goldhagen's views about the link between German people, German culture and anti-Semitism are controversial. This is illustrated in many reviews of the book. See, for example, Christopher R. Browning's comments in "Point of View: Human Nature, Culture, and the Holocaust," *The Chronicle of Higher Education*, October 18, 1996, p. A72. See also David Yanowski's review article, "Not a Hard Time Obeying Orders," *Books in Canada* (September 1996), pp. 31-33. Yanowski supports Goldhagen's challenge that "many people were not just passive bystanders, but either participated in or endorsed the Nazi genocidal enterprise" (p. 33).

12 Braham, *The Politics of Genocide*, p. 125.

13 Ibid., pp. 147-56.

14 Ibid., p. 155.

15 Ibid., pp. 194-95.

16 For observations by an onlooker, see Sandor Szenes, " 'Saving People Was Our Main Task . . .': An Interview with Reverend Jozsef Elias," in *Studies on the Holocaust in Hungary*, edited by Randolph L. Braham, Social Science Monographs, Boulder and the Csengeri Institute for Holocaust Studies of the Graduate School and University Center of the City University of

New York (New York: Columbia University Press, 1990), pp. 18-19. For a discussion of "obsessional prejudices," such as anti-Semitism, see Elisabeth Young-Bruehl, *The Anatomy of Prejudices* (Cambridge: Harvard University Press, 1996), pp. 459-68.

17 The relationship between anti-Semitism in Germany and its evolution in other countries is explained by Goldhagen in detail. Goldhagen believes that German anti-Semitism was unique because National Socialism was voted into power by the people of Germany in a way that it was not in other countries including, of course, Hungary.

18 See Braham, *The Politics of Genocide*, Vol. 2, pp. 820-50.

Other Books in the Life Writing Series Published by Wilfrid Laurier University Press

Haven't Any News: Ruby's Letters from the Fifties
Edited by Edna Staebler
with an Afterword by Marlene Kadar
1995 / x + 165 pp. / ISBN 0-88920-248-6

"I Want to Join Your Club": Letters from Rural Children, 1900-1920
Edited by Norah L. Lewis
with a Preface by Neil Sutherland
1996 / xii + 250 pp. (30 b&w photos) / ISBN 0-88920-260-5

And Peace Never Came
Elisabeth M. Raab
with Historical Notes by Marlene Kadar
1996 / x + 196 pp. (12 b&w photos, map) / ISBN 0-88920-281-8